GOD'S WORD REVISITED

Copyright Mr. C. J. Tibbert.
No part of this book may be reproduced in any form without permission in writing from the author unless the purpose is to spread the word of God in which case permission is freely given.

GOD'S WORD REVISITED

BY

C. J. TIBBERT

CONTENTS.

Page number

1. Preface   4.

2. .Part one.   7.

The Old Testament in chronological order as seen through the eyes of the main Bible characters.

3. Part two.   117.

The New Testament – as told by those present.

4. Part three.   185.

Answers to difficult questions and insights on doctrine.

Preface

If ever a book was born in prayer (particularly parts one and two) it is this one! Let me explain. The Church I attend has had three house groups up and running now for a number of years and our Sunday evening service is often conducted by elders, invited visitors, one of the Church organisations (e.g. the Guild, youth groups etc.) and on occasions by one of the house groups. I am privileged to lead one of these house groups and was wondering what we could organise if and when our turn came round to once again conduct an evening service. As the season was almost over (the evening service is suspended during the summer months) I thought we would have several months to prepare a format.

One Friday, while in prayer during my early morning quiet time, I confessed that I had no idea what our group would arrange when we were next asked to take the evening meeting. Before the prayer was finished I knew exactly what we were going to do! I was excited at the thought and thanked God for the inspiration. We would base our next service on four characters from the Bible and allow them to tell their story in their own words – as if they had each sent us a letter to explain their lives. The excitement continued all day and on returning home from work on Friday evening, I sat down and wrote continuously for three hours - not even pausing for a refreshment! After the three hours, which just flew by, I had Ruth, Esther, Mary the mother of Jesus, and Jairus, all telling their stories on paper. At least, I reasoned, the house group will be ready when called upon next season. That was on Friday evening! On Sunday morning, after Church, the lady who controls the rota for the evening services, came running after me and said, "Chris, is there any chance that your group could do an evening service in three weeks?" Why was I surprised? A smile spread across my face as I told her what had happened on Friday. She gave me a hug!

I asked one of my friends and neighbour, a devout Christian, to read over the manuscript and while he was reading it the thought came to me that it might be a good idea to write a book where the main characters of the Bible told their own story. When he had finished reading he said "You should write a book of Bible characters!" When you feel God is telling you to do something you had better do it! Right?

The evening service was well received and within days the idea continued to develop. I realised that the entire history contained within the Bible could be covered in a very interesting way if the innermost thoughts of the main Biblical characters were presented in chronological order.

How did Eve feel when she was tempted to eat the forbidden fruit and what did she think when she realised she had been tricked into opening the door to evil? How did Hannah feel, being mocked because she could not have children? And then when God blessed her with Samuel what were her thoughts on handing him over to Eli for temple duties? And the man born blind. How did he feel when he was able to see for the first time? What did Barabbas think, waiting to be executed and then finding himself released and watching Jesus die in his place?

Of course, it is not possible to cover every character in the Holy Book but those who are covered present the essential flow of His Story. However, one person not telling his story is Jesus Himself. Somehow I felt it would be almost blasphemous to presume to write Christ's innermost thoughts so He is missing from the list while being the cornerstone of all the others.

Part three of the book contains insights into controversies which cause consternation to many believers and hopefully the answers given will open minds to the truthfulness of the faith.

However, none of the facts contained in this work disagree with Biblical doctrine and I hope that some of the questions people ask may be answered within its cover.

My purpose in writing this book is not to try to replace the Bible but to whet the appetite for more of God's word; to show that the Holy Bible is not deadly boring but is alive and full of interest and if this book causes someone to decide to spend more time reading the scriptures I will be well pleased.

Please note that unless otherwise stated all Bible quotations are from the Good News Bible.

GOD'S WORD REVISITED - PART ONE.

THE OLD TESTAMENT REVEALED IN CHRONOLOGICAL ORDER AS SEEN THROUGH THE EYES OF THE MAIN BIBLE CHARACTERS.

		PAGE NUMBER
1.	ADAM	9.
2.	EVE	12.
3.	NOAH	15.
4.	ABRAHAM	18.
5.	ISAAC	22.
6.	JACOB	25.
7.	JOSEPH	28.
8.	MIRIAM	32.
9.	MOSES	35.
10.	AARON	38.
11.	BALAAM	41.
12.	JOSHUA	44.
13.	RAHAB	47.
14.	DEBORAH	50.

15. GIDEON	53.
16. JEPHTHAH	56.
17. SAMSON	59.
18. RUTH	62.
19. JOB	65.
20. HANNAH	68.
21. ELI	71.
22. SAMUEL	74.
23. DAVID	77.
24. NATHAN	80.
25. SOLOMON	83.
26. JEROBOAM	86.
27. JONAH	89.
28. ELIJAH	92.
29. ELISHA	96.
30. HEZEKIAH	99.
31. JOSIAH	102.
32. DANIEL	105.
33. EZRA	109.
34. ESTHER	111.
35. NEHEMIAH	114.

ADAM

I was amazed when God told me that He had made the whole of the universe in six days; each day representing the vast period of time taken to bring about the different stages of creation. He made me, Adam, in His image on the sixth day and considered that I was the peak of His creation. On the seventh day He rested. It was wonderful living with God in the garden paradise called Eden and I was pleased when He decided to create another one of each of the species of animals and birds and brought them to me so that I could give them names.

However, God knew that it would be good for me to have someone of my own kind as a companion and so He created Eve. She was beautiful and I took her as my wife. I loved the Lord as the Almighty and all knowing God but I loved Eve as an equal. You will no doubt be of the opinion that we should have been perfectly happy living in a paradise with the presence of such a caring God in our lives and we were - for a while! He hadn't burdened us with many constraints but, nevertheless, we managed to disobey Him by eating the fruit of the one tree in the garden which had been forbidden to us. As a result we were banished from the garden and life became much tougher!

Our first child, Cain, was born - the first fully human baby ever to be born on earth and we had great hopes for him but as he grew up he seemed to develop an attitude problem! Abel, our second son was born soon after. He honoured God and respected his parents.

When they were old enough the time came for them to make an offering to the Creator God. Abel who looked after the animals, selected the very first lamb born to one of his sheep. He was excited about the idea and took great delight in bringing this lamb, which he truly prized, to God as a token of his love and devotion. Cain, who farmed the land, felt that one lot of grain was much the same as any other and took no particular care to bring the best of his crops to God as his offering. As a result, God looked favourably upon the offering presented by Abel but with disdain upon that of Cain. It should have been a lesson to Cain but I was sad to see that he did not react well to that. In fact he was furious and became jealous of Abel. I was even sadder when I learned that Cain had arranged to meet Abel in the fields, picked a quarrel with him and killed him!

God knew what had happened and ordered Cain to leave our country. He also put a mark on him so that anyone meeting Cain in the future would know that God was dealing with the punishment and that they were not to take matters into their own hands. Eve and I felt that we had lost two sons over this incident and grieved for a long time. Our third son was a fine young man we named Seth and we had many other children after him.

God had made us, initially, genetically perfect and the corruption of our sin had not yet worked its degradation on our genes and so we lived for a very long time and our descendants were able to interbreed with no problems of malformation either mentally or physically. For example, I lived for 930 years and one of Seth's descendants, a man named Methuselah lived for 969 years which is longer than any other human being has ever lived on earth.

Unfortunately, my descendants were more interested in their own well-being than in observing the will of God and sin became prevalent over all the land. It saddened me greatly to see this happen because I felt responsible, for it was through me that evil had been able to enter our world. Sometimes I would look back with a touch of nostalgia at the joy and innocence we experienced in the garden of Eden before our disobedience and feel that I robbed all of humanity of an ideal relationship with God.

Now, of course, I realise that God had the perfect contingency plan in sending to earth His only begotten Son Jesus Christ who by his death on the cross undid the effect of my sin and took the punishment which each one of us humans deserves. It is plain to me that everyone can now be cleansed of the stains of sin by accepting the sacrifice which Christ made on our behalf. Of course the great plan of salvation is conditional upon a sincere desire for forgiveness and a determination to avoid sin in the future.

In spite of what I did, it is wonderful to know that Jesus has opened the doors of Heaven and awaits with arms outstretched to welcome all who come to Him. Thank you Lord!

EVE

I can't tell you anything about my childhood. No! It's not that I can't remember it's just that I was never a child! You see my name is Eve and I was created by God as a fully formed woman. The first fully human woman ever and I became the mother of the whole human race. My husband, Adam, was created just before me and we learned everything from God Himself.

We were living in a most beautiful garden called Eden where there was a plentiful supply of fruit all year round and we were allowed to eat the fruit of any tree in the garden - except one! Our Creator described its fruit as being the knowledge of good and evil and told us we would die if we ate it and so we were careful to avoid it. It did look very tasty though!

The other fruits in the garden were delicious but I kept wondering what the forbidden fruit would taste like. Adam didn't seem to bother. He was happy tending the garden, caring for the animals and enjoying my company and we both loved being in God's presence. The weather was beautiful too with an occasional cloud casting its shadow and shielding us from the heat of the sun. A shadow also fell over our bliss and I was to blame for it!

The animals in the garden wouldn't do us any harm, but there was a certain cunning about the snake. I did not realise that he was the adversary of our Creator. He saw me looking at the forbidden tree. "Go on" he said, "taste its fruit." I explained that God had said we would die if we did. "He's just saying that - you won't die. God knows that you will become just like Him and have the knowledge of good and evil. He doesn't want you to be equal to Him - go on taste it!"

I wondered if God did have an ulterior motive - and the fruit was so tempting! It was in my hand before I realised it and I tasted it! It was lovely - just as the others fruits were but with the added flavour of being forbidden! I waited to see if I would die on the spot - I didn't! Adam must try it too I thought. When I told Adam what the snake had said he was doubtful but he ate the fruit just to please me.

Then we realised we were naked and stitched fig leaves together to wear in an act of modesty. For the first time we were both unsure of our behaviour. What could we do and what couldn't we do? Before, walking in God's presence, everything was clear - now we were confused and afraid of what God would say.

That evening He called Adam who had been hiding from Him. God knew that Adam had eaten the forbidden fruit and asked him why. I cowered away, embarrassed, as Adam explained that I had encouraged him to eat it. God then turned to me and asked me to explain. I rather spluttered out the answer that the snake had beguiled me into it. God was not pleased that disobedience had been introduced to this paradise. He denounced the snake and told me that we women would, from then on, give birth to children in great pain. He also allowed weeds and thorns to grow and told us that because of our action we would have to work hard to produce the food for our sustenance. I also realised that we had lost our immortality and that in time we would surely die. God banished us from our garden paradise.

Taking a bite of that fruit was certainly not worth it but as I have discovered, disobeying God's word is never worth it! I can tell you when I was giving birth to Cain, my first child, I really cursed the snake for enticing me to eat that fruit. The pain of labour was something I had never expected.

That was not the end of the troubles because when we disobeyed God we opened the door to evil. If only we could go back in time - I would never take that fruit again - but it's too late. How easy it is to

13

throw away something precious for the pleasure of the moment - and how foolish!

NOAH

I lived on earth at a time when evil flourished in the land and there appeared to be no one who observed the word of God. It was a disgusting period when humanity dredged the depths of depravity and violence was rife. I felt as if I was the only one who lived in obedience to the Lord and tried to emulate Enoch, one of my most honoured ancestors - a man who walked with God all his life. In fact, he was the first man to be taken into Heaven without tasting death. He was descended from Adam's son, Seth, and his example and reputation were my guidelines but in my wicked generation I stood out as target for mockery - an object of ridicule.

The ridicule increased when I started to build a large sailing vessel. "Noah has finally cracked." I heard their scornful derision, but I knew better. You see, it was God Himself who had warned me that He was about to send a flood over all the earth to destroy the wickedness which was so prevalent. He told me to construct an ark and gave me instructions regarding its form and dimensions. In the future most people would come to think of the ark as being not much bigger than a house boat but in reality it was about 130 metres in length and had three decks! A truly mammoth task but I worked at it day and night until it was finished and then I coated it with tar, inside and out, to make it watertight as God had instructed.

He also instructed that a male and female of every animal were to be brought into the ark - one pair of certain animals but seven pairs of birds and some other animals. It was difficult rounding them all up but with God's help I managed. My wife, three sons and their wives were also brought on board as was an ample supply of food.

Then came the first drops of rain - not too heavy at the start but we settled in and waited. We heard the rain become torrential. At first the ground outside became muddy but before long the rivers burst their banks and flooded the land. Shortly afterwards we felt the ark sway. We were afloat! I organised everyone to check every part of the ark for leaks. There were none!

It rained constantly for forty days and nights causing the waters to rise above the mountain tops and every being living on the land was destroyed. The rain stopped suddenly! For forty days we had heard its continuous pounding on our boat. Then Silence! Our world had become a universal sea and we were floating on it. Would the water level ever go down? Well, it did, but it took time! We lived in the ark for a long, long year!!

The animals had caused us little bother - in fact, I wondered if God had put them into a state of suspended animation but after all that time we were eager to get out of the ark and into the fresh air. Then we felt the ark go aground so I sent out a raven to see if there might be dry land but the raven gave us no indication of that. Later I sent out a dove but there was no dry land because the dove returned to us. Seven days later I sent it out again and this time it came back with an olive leaf in its beak - a hopeful sign that the waters were receding rapidly I thought. Another seven days passed and I sent the dove out once again. This time it did not come back. The flood had gone! The joy of stepping out of that ark and into the sunshine can only be imagined! The animals too enjoyed their freedom!

God told us to go out and multiply so that our numbers would spread throughout the land. He gave us rules which we were to observe in our general living, in our relationships and in our consumption of food, and the families of my sons, Shem, Ham and Japheth grew and spread over the land as God had commanded.

I built an altar and offered a sacrifice to the Lord which He accepted. He made a covenant with me that He would never again send a flood to destroy all living beings and as a sign of that covenant He put a beautiful rainbow in the sky and said that each time He saw the rainbow He would remember His promise - I did too, for the rest of my life!

Some may think God was cruel in destroying life but I think He was really showing us that He will not tolerate evil and that one day sin will be completely destroyed.

ABRAHAM

Almost three hundred years after the great flood I, a descendant of Noah's son Shem, was born and was named Abram. I lived in the city of Ur in Babylonia until my father Terah moved us all north to Haran. We were a fairly wealthy family and had many slaves and so, soon established ourselves in our new location. At that time people believed in a variety of gods and worshipping several at one time was common practise. That was when God Almighty spoke to me directly, telling me to go the land of Canaan. I took my wife Sarai, my nephew Lot, my slaves and my cattle and settled in Canaan as the Lord had commanded.

In spite of the fact that my behaviour was sometimes a little less than exemplary, God promised that the land as far as the eye could see would belong to my descendants. As Sarai was unable to have children, that seemed unlikely but maybe He knew something I didn't.

After a sojourn in Egypt we continued to prosper and the number of our animals grew so large that Lot and I decided the time had come to go our separate ways. Lot went to a city called Sodom while I set up home in Hebron. A little later I was shocked to learn that Sodom had been looted and Lot taken captive by a band of raiders. I selected three hundred of my best men to give chase. We caught up with the group, rescued Lot and confiscated the loot. On the way back home I met Melchizedek, king of Salem and priest of the Most High God. I recognised a special anointing of this man and when he gave me his blessing I gave him one tenth of all we had captured. The remainder I returned to the king of Sodom.

Again the Lord covenanted with me that my descendants would be great in number and possess the land but still Sarai was childless. After all the years of hoping for a baby, Sarai had become resigned to the fact that she was now too old to have children but she knew how much I wanted to be a father and so she suggested that I take her Egyptian slave girl, Hagar, to be my concubine. In those days polygamy was practised by many who could afford it and a concubine was a slave who was given many of the rights of a normal wife. Hagar soon became pregnant which multiplied Sarai's distress. Firstly, she realise that it was she and not me who could not have children and secondly, Hagar used her new found status to look down on Sarai with contempt, especially after she gave birth to a son who was named Ishmael.

Yet again God confirmed that my descendants would be so numerous that they would be regarded as nations. I presumed He meant through Ishmael but He said that Sarai was to be blessed and would have a son who was to be named Isaac. Now Sarai was well past child bearing age but, as I learned, nothing is impossible for God. He told me that from then on my name would be Abraham which in Hebrew sounds like "Ancestor of many nations" and Sarai was to be called by the Hebrew name for princess - Sarah! The Covenant was also formalised at that time and as its sign, the rite of circumcision was introduced. I, and all the males in my household were circumcised that day and all my descendants and those who consider themselves to be under this covenant have been circumcised ever since.

Sarah could not contain her laughter when I told her she was to have a son. I can't be sure if it was scornful disbelief or joy which prompted the outburst but whatever it was she did give birth to Isaac about a year later.

Meanwhile the Lord was displeased with the evil which was so widespread in Sodom and its neighbouring town of Gomorrah and informed me of His intention to destroy these two towns. I pleaded with Him and suggested that it wasn't right to destroy the good with the bad and if there were even fifty good men in Sodom it should not be destroyed. God told me that He would not destroy the city if there were fifty good men there. I pushed my luck and tried for forty. He agreed! I kept pushing until I got to ten and God said that if there were ten righteous men he would spare Sodom. I was pretty sure there would be ten good men in a place like that - but I was wrong!

Lot had offered hospitality to two of God's messengers but the men of Sodom were consumed by passion - they wanted to rape the visitors! Lot tried to protect his guests but the Sodomites persisted until the power of God struck them with blindness. Because he defended the strangers, God decided to spare Lot and his family and told them to hurry out of the town. As they fled God sent down burning sulphur destroying Sodom and Gomorrah. Lot's wife paused to look back and was turned into a pillar of salt. The others reached the village of Zoar in safety.

Sarah was overjoyed when Isaac was born but her relationship with Hagar deteriorated even further and eventually she insisted that Hagar must be sent away together with Ishmael. Then God said something which really shocked me. He told me to offer my son Isaac to Him as a sacrifice. Yes - He was saying that I had to slay Isaac in the same way that we did the animals we had sacrificed from the time of our ancestors! Surely not! He couldn't mean that! I got no indication that He was joking! This was undoubtedly the greatest and worst test He had confronted me with! Isaac was my son of the Covenant - he was precious to me! I didn't dare tell Sarah! God told me to take Isaac to a mountain in the land of Moriah where the deed was to take place. Just for a moment I thought of saying no; but how could I defy the God who had given me so much and whose power I had seen in action? He was a God I knew I could trust and even if this made no sense to me I would have to carry out His command.

After travelling for three days we arrived at the designated spot where I built an altar for the sacrifice and got everything ready. Isaac who was old enough by that time to understand that a sacrifice was about to take place asked the whereabouts of the animal we were going to offer as the sacrifice. My heart was breaking as I replied "The Lord will provide". I bound Isaac and placed him on the altar and as I raised the knife and steeled myself to plunge it into his body these thoughts went through my mind: Would God bring him back to life?; Would Sarah be able to have another son? Had I sinned so greatly that the Lord had decided to cancel the Covenant? What would Sarah say? Before I could bring the knife down on him the angel of the Lord called my name and told me not to harm the boy. He said that I had shown my obedience even to the point where I had been prepared to offer my precious son to Him. My relief was beyond words! Then I saw a ram which was trapped by the horns in some bushes - God had provided the sacrifice!

The Lord had shown me just how painful it would be to give my son as a sacrifice to Him - and as I later realised it was no less painful for Him to give His son as a sacrifice for all humanity!

ISAAC

An incident in my boyhood left me traumatised for weeks and gave me nightmares for months. It was one occasion when my father, Abraham, said to me, "Isaac, get ready we're going on a trip to the land of Moriah."

I always enjoyed going on these trips so I very quickly got organised. We set off and after three days, reached our destination. My father built an altar which I knew was for making a sacrifice to God. Then he tied me up and I truly believed he was going to offer me as the sacrifice! I was in terror as he raise the knife but at the last moment he stopped and set me free. I was always a little hesitant after that when he suggested going on a trip. However, he proved his love for me over and over again and soon regained my trust. His love for me was great indeed, but his love for God was supreme!

When my mother, Sarah died, father and I were in mourning for a long time. He bought a special piece of land which contained a cave at Machpelah. This is where he buried my mother.

At that point he decided it was time for me to marry and so he sent his oldest and most trusted servant back up north to the land of his birth in search of a young woman from his own people. Apparently he did not want me to marry a Canaanite girl. God had probably told him so for it seems that God communed with him regularly just like a friend.

I waited with anticipation to see what kind of girl, if any, our old servant would bring back. Would she be fat or thin, tall or small, ugly (I hoped not) or beautiful? At last I saw the group return and there she was! What a vision! She was beautiful! Rebecca - that was her name! She was not only lovely on the outside, she was a delight to talk to also. Soon we fell in love and she became my wife.

We were happy together and eventually, in answer to prayer, Rebecca became pregnant. She had a difficult time, particularly in the final months when it was discovered that she was carrying twins. The two unborn babies seemed to struggle against each other in the womb and God told us that the first one to be born would serve the second and that they would become two rival nations.

When they were born they certainly were not identical twins in fact two more different brothers would be hard to imagine. The first one we named Esau and he was covered in a fuzz of red hair while Jacob, the second, was smooth skinned. Esau grew up to be a first class hunter who loved the outdoors and could be described as a real man's man which pleased me. Jacob, on the other hand, was quieter, sensitive, more thoughtful and was a delight to Rebecca.

I was annoyed at Esau one day, though, because he showed such little regard for the privileges our traditions bestowed upon the first born son. Jacob had been cooking and Esau came in feeling ravenous. He asked Jacob for some food and Jacob replied that he would give Esau the food on condition that the rights of the first-born son would be passed to him. Esau vowed agreement. I found it very disappointing to learn that he thought his birthright was worth only a plate of food.

Some time later a famine drove us to the land of the Philistines where we settled in Gerar. In spite of the fact that I was not entirely truthful to the people there, God blessed me greatly and multiplied my crops, slaves and livestock and I became very rich and powerful. Much to my regret, Esau married two Hittite girls named Judith and Basemath both of whom caused no end of trouble to Rebecca and me.

By that time I was very old and had become blind and felt that I should give my final blessing to my sons. Although Esau had sold his birthright, he was still entitled to the blessing belonging to the first-born son. I told him to hunt an animal, kill it and cook me a meal and then I would give him his rightful blessing. As I learned later, Rebecca had overheard the conversation and wanted that special blessing for her favourite son - Jacob. She cooked a meal, dressed Jacob in Esau's clothes and put goatskin on his arms to make him feel hairy like Esau. Jacob brought me the meal pretending to be Esau and asked for the first born's blessing. His voice was that of Jacob but his clothes smelled of Esau and his arms were not smooth as I knew Jacob's were and so I gave him the blessing belonging to the first-born son.

A little later, Esau came in and I realised I had been deceived. I trembled all over for the shock, I suppose, nearly killed me. Esau begged me for his blessing but once a blessing is given it cannot be taken back so I gave Esau the best blessing I could in the circumstances. He, of course, was incandescent with rage and denounced Jacob for cheating him twice; first from his birthright and now from his blessing.

Rebecca feared for Jacob's safety! She suggested sending Jacob to seek a wife in Mesopatamia where Abraham, Jacob's grandfather, came from, for she said she could not bear it if he married a Hittite woman. I agreed and Jacob went to find a wife, and safety from Esau's wrath, in Mesopatamia

I lived for a long time after that; long enough to learn that both my sons prospered greatly and and been reconciled. Jacob, in fact had twelve sons who were the founders of the twelve tribes of Israel!

As I pondered all of these matters I became aware that God can take anything, good or bad, and bring out the best from it as He did with my sons! Praise His name!!

JACOB

I travelled from Gerar where I had been living to Haran in order to find a wife from among my parents' people. Well, that was part of the reason - the other part was that I had to escape the wrath of my brother because I had been guilty of sharp practice in depriving him of his rights as the first-born son and of his patriarchal blessing from our father. You see, my name is Jacob and my brother is Esau – we were twin brothers in fact to our father and mother, Isaac and Rebecca.

On the way to Haran I had a vivid dream where I saw a ladder extending from earth to heaven with angels climbing up and down. A voice spoke telling me that I would have many descendants and that the land on which I lay would one day belong to my children. I named the place Bethel.

When I arrived in Haran I saw a girl who had come to water her sheep at a well. She turned out to be Rachel and her father was my mother's brother. Rachel was so beautiful that I could hardly take my eyes off her. She took me to her father - my uncle Laban and after a cordial welcome we agreed that I should work for him and my wages for seven years' labour would be the hand of Rachel in marriage.

The seven years passed quickly because I had well and truly fallen in love with her. However, at the marriage, I was deceived and after the wedding festival found that I had married Leah - Rachel's older sister. Now Leah had her good qualities but was no match for her sister. Laban tried to explain away the deception by saying that custom demanded that the older daughter should be the first to marry. He then said that Rachel could be my wife also, after one

25

week, provided that I agreed to work for him for another seven years. Such was my love for her that I agreed.

Leah gave birth to Reuben and then to Simeon, Levi and Judah while Rachel appeared unable to have any children. Years passed and Rachel gave me her handmaiden, Bilhah, thinking that she could have children through her. Bilhah gave birth to Dan and Naphtali. Not to be outdone, Leah gave me her handmaiden, Zilpah, through whom I had Gad and Asher. Then Leah herself gave birth again firstly to Issachar followed by Zebulum and then to a girl we called Dinah. Finally the Lord blessed Rachel and she gave birth to Joseph and at a later date to Benjamin.

As I continued to work for Laban we came to the agreement that, in future, I should be given certain of the animals born in the herds. I suppose sharp practice was always in my nature for I arranged that the best of the animals being born belonged to me. In the end the Lord told me to take what was mine and return to my father. I did so feeling very apprehensive about the reception I would get from Esau.

In advance of our party I sent gifts to my brother who came to meet us and for the first time that I can remember we shared true brotherly love with each other. Thanks be to God that we were a real family again! He noticed that I was limping for on the previous night I had to wrestle with a messenger from God and would not release him until he blessed me. Eventually he did so but also struck the hollow of my thigh causing damage to the joint which never healed.

I was happy to settle there in a place called Shechem and to watch my family grow up. Unfortunately things don't run smoothly all the time for one day my daughter, Dinah, was raped by a man named Shechem, the son of a ruler of the Hivites. He decided he would like to marry Dinah but my sons said that he and his people would have to be circumcised first. He agreed and while they were all still sore from the circumcision Simeon and Levi took swords and in revenge for what had been done to Dinah they killed them all.

I feared reprisals and was pleased when God told me to go to live in Bethel for a while. I did and He blessed me once again confirming that the land would belong to my children and that from then on I should be known as Israel. The time came for us to move on and it was then that the great heartbreak of my life happened. That was when Rachel, in giving birth to Benjamin died in the process. We buried her on the road to Ephrath which was later known as Bethlehem. I mourned for her greatly and missed her intensely but tragedy had not finished its work. Joseph who was the apple of my eye, sometimes riled his brothers but he was a special boy and you can imagine how grieved I was when his brothers came home one day with the coat I had made him. It was covered in blood! I assumed he had been killed by a wild animal.

Many years later there was a severe famine in the land and I had to send some of my children to Egypt to buy food. After the second such journey they came home and excitedly told me the unbelievably good news that not only was Joseph alive but that he was the mighty Pharaoh's right hand man! In fact he had asked us to come and live with him in Egypt! When we did we were treated as honoured guests and given choice land to live on.

My life it seems was made up of something one of my descendants was later to write: - a time to be happy and a time to be sad; a time to laugh and a time to cry. In Egypt we were happy and laughed!

JOSEPH

I didn't mean to appear to be a brash, superior and cocky youth but that is exactly the way my other eleven brothers saw me. I would hear them say things such as;- "That Joseph is an idle good for nothing dreamer" and see anger written all over their faces. My natural exuberance sometimes overruled discretion but it made me my father's favourite. That, coupled with the fact that my mother, Rachel, was the best loved of my father's wives, caused him to spoil me a little much to the annoyance of my brothers. He even made me a long coat with materials of different colours which was eye catching in luxury and beauty.

The last straw, as far as the other eleven were concerned, was when I told them about two dreams I had, both of which indicated that one day they would all bow down to pay honour and homage to me. Perhaps it was rash of me to tell them about the dreams because my brothers were filled with indignation and started to look for ways to punish me.

One day my father sent me to check on their safety as they had been away for some time tending our flock. When I caught up with them there was a rude awakening in store for me! They were discussing how they were going to kill me! Reuben my eldest brother (actually he was my half brother as they all were except the youngest, Benjamin, whose mother was also Rachel) felt a little more compassionate. He said I should be placed in a dried out well. He was really planning just to teach me a lesson and to rescue me later. I had been in the well for some time when I heard a noise above. They had come back to pull me out - they weren't so bad after all I thought but it was a short-lived thought! On being pulled from the well, I noticed with apprehension a band of Midianite traders nearby and heard my brothers bargain with them. They were about to sell me, and Reuben was not there to apply common sense! Twenty pieces of silver was my price! Oh, how my father was to grieve for me when he was told I had been killed!

I was taken to Egypt where I was sold on as a slave to a man called Potiphar who was one of the king's officers and captain of the palace guard. For a while I was homesick and missed my family; - yes even those traitorous brothers but things could have been worse. As slaves go I was treated well and responded in a manor which earned respect. In a short time I was given responsibilities and it was not long before Potiphar put me in charge of his entire household. I was still young, well-built and, so they told me, good-looking and I noticed that Potiphar's wife glanced in my direction a lot. Sometimes when no one else was around she allowed her robe to slip revealing more flesh than modesty should permit. Perhaps it was accidental I reasoned, but in time it became quite clear that it was not. She talked to me in the most seductive way and suggested that we should go to bed. How could I betray my master, Potiphar, and offend my God? I refused her offer! Driven by lust she made the suggestion day after day and finally, realising she would not get her way, falsely accused me of trying to rape her. Potiphar, of course, believed her and I was put in prison.

It seemed tragic at the time but God was using these trying experiences to mould my character. No longer was I brash and cocky; the rough edges of overconfidence and bragging were being knocked off and I still trusted in the God of my fathers. I had learned to try to make the best of any situation and soon became trusted by the prison guards. In fact, they used me to run the prison for them.

One night, two of my fellow prisoners had vivid dreams which disturbed them both. I explained that God had given me the gift of interpretation of dreams and told them what their dreams meant. My explanations both came true and one of the men was reinstated as the king's wine steward.

For two more years life in the prison proceeded as normal and then, unexpectedly, I was taken to the king. He had had two dreams which preyed powerfully on his mind. Not one of his advisors or magicians could tell him what they meant. His wine steward remembered how I had interpreted his dream accurately and informed the king who summoned me. The king's dreams meant that there were to be seven years of plentiful harvests followed by seven years of the most severe famine - so severe that many people would be in danger of death from starvation. My natural exuberance was still part of me and I continued to tell the king what he should do:- appoint someone to organise the collecting and storing of grain during the good years so that there would be ample in reserve for the lean years. The detailed plan I gave him made him decide that I was the man for the job and he made me Governor of Egypt. I travelled all over the country in that capacity and in every city, organised huge stores of grain over the seven years of plenty.

Then the famine started as predicted and slowly people from all over Egypt and neighbouring lands were affected. Egyptians and foreigners alike came to me begging for food and I opened the storehouses to sell supplies to them. Ten men from my old town in Canaan came in desperation asking for food. They did not recognise me for it had been about thirteen years since I had seen my brothers and the last thing they would have expected was to see "that little pest Joseph" as second in command over the whole of mighty Egypt! I did not reveal my identity to them and although I understood them perfectly well, I arranged to talk to them through an interpreter. I asked about their family and was delighted to learn that my father was still alive and that Benjamin, my youngest brother, had stayed at home with him. Partly because I wanted to teach them a lesson and partly because I wanted revenge, I pretended to believe they were spies and had them put in prison for three days. Then I released them and told them they were allowed to buy corn but in order to prove they were genuine one of them would have to remain in prison while the others took back the provisions to their starving families. They were then to return to Egypt with the youngest brother. They agreed to this and I chose to hold Simeon in prison. Thinking that I would not understand their language they started talking among themselves. It was then I learned that Reuben had tried to persuade the others to do me no harm all those years ago and was shocked that day when he returned to the group and found me missing. They still did not know who I was. I sent them on their way putting the money they had paid for the corn in each of their sacks.

Eventually they came back returning the original money and with additional funds to purchase more corn. I reunited them with Simeon and when I saw Benjamin, love welled up in my heart. I had to leave the room in case they saw the tears in my eyes. I played a little trickery on them like a cat playing with a mouse and made them terrified but I couldn't keep it up. I told them who I was! Delight? No fear on their faces! What revenge would I wreck on them they wondered, but I wept openly and hugged each one in turn. The king learned of my brothers' arrival and invited them to bring their families to live in Egypt. I was overjoyed when they all came to join me and it was wonderful to see my father again. The years of struggle and mourning for me had aged him but he was so happy to know I was alive and to be with me again. My family were given the best land to settle in. They were happy in Egypt and our descendants prospered and multiplied greatly.

Although my brothers had meant evil by selling me, God changed it into good. But then doesn't He always.?

MIRIAM

When Joseph, our famous ancestor, was taken to Egypt and became second in importance only to the Pharaoh, the Egyptians welcomed his family and gave them choice land to live on. Over hundreds of years Joseph had gradually been forgotten while the descendants of his family had grown greatly in numbers to the point where the Egyptians felt threatened. The preferential treatment willingly given during Joseph's time had been long since withdrawn and we were treated like slaves by the Egyptians.

In order to protect themselves from what they saw as "that rapidly expanding foreign race" the Pharaoh issued a desperate and highly iniquitous command:- that all the baby boys born to us Hebrews were to be killed! Imagine the despair which spread through our families! Having the little baby boys taken from their mothers and murdered! While this rule was in force, my mother, Jochebed, gave birth to a little baby boy whom we named Moses, a little brother for me, Miriam and my other brother, Aaron.

He was such an attractive baby! How could we let him be killed? Desperate times call for desperate measures! We came up with a plan which was quite illogical and with only an outside chance of success. We placed Moses in a basket which we had made watertight and put it in the river Nile hoping he would be found downstream. Our wildest hopes were realised when the basket was discovered by the Pharaoh's daughter while she was bathing. As soon as she saw him she picked him up and immediately fell in love with the baby. There and then she decided to rear him as a prince of Egypt.

It may have been a dangerous thing to do but I took a gamble and approached the royal party. When I suggested that a little baby like him should be properly weaned, the princess agreed and instructed me to get one of the Hebrew women to wet nurse him. I, of course, brought my mother which meant that Moses was weaned by his own mother in the luxury of the royal palace. He grew up with all the trimmings of a prince, but he knew he was one of us – Hebrew, not Egyptian.

When he had grown to be a young man, anger boiled over in him as he witnessed an Egyptian guard ill-treat one of the Hebrew slaves and, after a tussle, Moses killed the guard. He realised he had been seen committing the murder so he fled to the land of Midian for safety. The next time I saw him was many years later when he came back to give the Pharaoh the message that God wanted His people, the Hebrews, to be set free. Understandably the request was refused. God, however, sent a series of disasters upon the Egyptians, each one worse than the preceding, culminating with the death of the first born son in each Egyptian home.

As a result of this final act, Pharaoh, fearing further reprisals from our God, allowed us to go free, some 430 years after Joseph's family had originally settled in Egypt. Moses, under instruction from the Lord, then led around one million of us into the desert. I was happy to think that this great man was my little brother and we could all see that God was with him. However, human nature being what it is, many soon forgot the strain and oppression of life under the Egyptians and started to complain about the harsh life in the desert. Even Aaron and I slipped into critical mode when Moses married a Cushite woman. We questioned his authority to lead us and his willingness to obey the Lord's commands. God gave me the answer in a drastic way - I was immediately struck with leprosy. Although I had been very aggressive to him, Moses prayed for me and told me that God said that I should be punished by having that dreaded disease for seven days. I had to stay outside the camp but after seven days I was completely healed!

God did some amazing things for us such as :- parting the Red sea; providing water from rocks; giving us a daily supply of a food we named 'Manna', which in Hebrew means "What is it?", protecting us from any enemies and bringing quail for us to eat for a change. The Lord also gave Moses tablets containing the Ten Commandments and guided him throughout his life.

We wandered in the desert for forty years but because we had been disobedient from time to time none of the people of my generation, with the exception of two of our scouts who had desired to carry out the Lord's will, was allowed to enter the promised land. I was rather disappointed at that but took comfort from the fact that Moses was my brother - such a humble, receptive and yet strong man whom God was able to speak to face to face and work through him directly. Sometimes I wished that I could have been more like that!

MOSES

When I, Moses, was a baby I was placed in a basket and hidden in the river Nile in Egypt because the Egyptian midwives had been given orders to kill all the baby boys born to their Hebrew slaves. I was discovered by the Pharaoh's daughter who adopted me and brought me up as a prince of Egypt. However, I was aware of my Hebrew blood line and when I grew up and saw an Egyptian cruelly mistreat one of the Hebrews, I fought with him and, I am afraid, killed him. Although I had not intended that to happen I feared the consequences and ran away to Midian which was over the Red sea and across the Sinai desert.

It was there that I went to work, as a shepherd, for a man called Jethro and after a while he became my father-in-law as I married his daughter Zipporah and we had a son whom we named Gershom. One day while tending the sheep in the area of Mount Sinai I saw a truly magnificent sight - a bush was burning but it was not being consumed. I went to investigate and heard a voice call my name. There was no one around and the voice seemed to come from the bush! It spoke again saying He was the God of my ancestors and that I should take off my sandals for I was standing on Holy ground. Then He told me that His chosen people were being cruelly treated by the Egyptians and that I must go to the Pharaoh and tell him to release the Hebrew people and that I was to lead them out of Egypt. I expressed doubts about my ability to do that but He told me that He would display His mighty power through me and that Aaron, my brother, would assist me.

The Lord assured me that I would not be punished for my crime of murder and so I said farewell to Jethro, took my wife and family and set off for Egypt. The previous Pharaoh had died and the man I, at one time, regarded as a brother was in his place. He stubbornly refused to allow the Hebrews to leave even although Aaron and I gave evidence of God's power. I warned him that God would send plagues on Egypt but his answer was a firm "NO"!

God sent the plagues! First the river Nile and the canals and pools turned to blood and all the fish died. Then followed frogs; flies; the death of many animals; people developed huge boils; hail flattened the crops; locusts; darkness over the land after which the Pharaoh decided to let the people go! However, his remorse did not last long - before we could set off, he changed his mind! I informed him that God had yet another tribulation to send on him - every first born son in each Egyptian household would be slain by the angel of death. He refused to listen. God told me that the Hebrews should spread the blood of a lamb or goat on their door posts. We did as He said and the angel of death passed over those houses but every first born son of the Egyptians died that night! The Jewish celebration of Passover owes its origin to that event. Pharaoh let us go!!

We set out and had reached the Red sea when we discovered that Pharaoh had once again had a change of heart. He had sent his army to bring us back! Then God did an amazing thing He parted the sea - there were walls of water on both sides of us as we passed through on dry land. When we reached the other side the Egyptian soldiers started in after us. The walls of water came crashing down on top of them and they were drowned! We wandered through the wilderness, a group of over one million people, and under God's guidance came to the land of Canaan which is where God intended us to settle.

I sent scouts to check out the land. Two of them, Joshua and Caleb, came back with the report that as God was with us we should take the land but the others put fear into the hearts of our group causing them to reject the recommendation to enter Canaan. Their lack of faith meant that God would not permit any of our generation to enter Canaan and we had to wander in the wilderness for 40 years during which time I was given instructions about the priesthood and was told many rules for holy and healthy living and, of course, received the Ten Commandments which are the great fundamental rules forming the basis of all the others laws. In a nutshell they are as follows:-

1. Worship no other God but the Lord Almighty.

2. Make no idols or images and give no honour to these things.

3. Treat the Lord's name with the honour it is due.

4. Observe the Sabbath day as a day devoted to Him.

5. Give your father and mother the respect they deserve so that things will go well with you.

6. Do not commit murder.

7. Do not commit adultery.

8. Do not steal.

9. Do not say things which are not true about anyone.

10. Do not be filled with envious desire for anything belonging to someone else.

God also revealed plans from which we built the tabernacle and the sacred Covenant box symbolising the presence of the Lord and into which was placed the tablets containing the Ten Commandments. God did some wondrous things in those 40 years but it was a time of suffering also. Then the group did enter and take Canaan - the promised land! If only the people had had the faith of Joshua and Caleb, 40 years previously.

As I think about it I wonder - how many lives are spent in the wilderness of despair because they lack faith in Almighty God and fail to trust in His benevolent will.

AARON

I suppose there are two things I am remembered for above all others and one of them is my stick otherwise known as Aaron's rod. The other is that the Jewish priesthood is named after me - the Aaronic, or Levitical, priesthood. Firstly, sticks played a very important role in my life. There was the time when my younger brother, Moses, and I went to the king of Egypt and told him that God wanted him to set free the Israelite slaves who were also known as Hebrews. At that time I threw down the stick which had been given by God and it became a snake. The king, who was called the Pharaoh, brought in his magicians who by sleight of hand did the same thing producing snakes from other sticks. However, my snake swallowed theirs but Pharaoh was not convinced.

Then God instructed me to hold the stick over the river Nile and it turned to blood killing all the fish. Still Pharaoh would not budge. Then followed plagues of frogs and flies each of which was brought about by using the stick at God's command. Other plagues followed and eventually Pharaoh set our people free.

We escaped to the wilderness and at one point were desperate for drinking water. God told Moses to take my stick and strike a rock with it. As soon as he did water poured from the rock - enough to satisfy the entire group.

Then the Amalekites attacked us at Rephidim. Moses told Joshua to organise our men to do battle. He climbed to the top of a hill and held out the stick. Whenever his arms were raised we Israelites gained the upper hand but when he grew tired and lowered his arms we started to lose. Hur and I took a rock for him to sit on and held his arms aloft until our people won the battle.

There was another occasion I should mention when sticks were used for God's purposes. It was at the time when many in our party were complaining about everything including the leadership and the fact the the tribe of the Levites had been allocated the duties of the priesthood and care of the sacred items of worship. The Lord told Moses that the twelve tribes were each to give him a stick representing their tribe. My stick denoted the tribe of Levi. They were placed in front of the Covenant box and the following morning God showed which tribe He had chosen - my stick had sprouted, blossomed and produced a crop of almonds! End of the argument! The priests and all those who were to take care of the sacred items of worship were always to be selected from my tribe - the Levites! That is why the Jewish priesthood is called the Aaronic or Levitical priesthood.

The duty carried with it great responsibility and we were fully occupied in serving the Lord and therefore had no time to engage in income producing labour. And so it was that the Lord introduced the system of tithing, that is, that the other tribes gave one tenth of their income to fund us and the upkeep of the place of worship.

I was not always the best example to everyone, however, and on one occasion made God and Moses very angry. Moses had climbed Mount Sinai to speak to the Lord face to face and had been away for many days when the people suggested making a gold calf from their jewellery. I thought it might be a useful occupation and organised it but when it was complete they all started to sing and dance to its honour and I am afraid I joined in. In the end the party became a drunken orgy!

Moses came down from the mountain at that point and was furious at what we had done. It seemed to him that as soon as he went away, we forgot all about Almighty God and chose a god of our own making. He melted the gold calf, ground it to dust, mixed it with water and made us drink it. God's punishment for our having worshipped an idol was severe for the Levites put to death a portion of our numbers. 3000 people were slain that day! I felt ashamed of what I had done and asked forgiveness from God and from Moses. Thankfully I received forgiveness and have never made that mistake again for God made it quite clear that nothing that is not of God Himself should be given the honour, trust, love and faith that belongs to Him alone! Nothing!!

My earthly life came to an end on top of Mount Hor and Eleazar, my son, assumed my mantle of responsibility. He witnessed an incident which I now know was very significant. Our people were being attacked by poisonous snakes and many of them were dying. When Moses prayed to the Lord, he was told to make a snake of bronze and to lift it up on a pole so that everyone could see it. Remarkably, whenever the Israelites looked to the bronze snake, the venom of the snake-bites was nullified! I believe that it was a precursor of Jesus Christ, the son of God. For when He was raised up on the cross of crucifixion He took the sins of the world on His shoulders so that when anyone looks to Him, seeking forgiveness, the poison of their sins is nullified.

BALAAM

Don't think you have to be a paragon of virtue before the Lord will speak to you! He spoke to me so I know! My name is Balaam, son of Beor and I lived at Pethor, near the river Euphrates. My reputation as a man who had a personal acquaintance with God, was widespread and people relied on me to petition God whenever they wanted Him to act in their favour.

At the time when the Israelites were travelling through the wilderness, stories about surprising victories over their enemies filtered through the whole of the land and the populace were apprehensive whenever the Hebrew multitude approached their territory. King Balak of Moab was no exception! When he heard that the people of Israel were nearby, he was anxious for the safety of the Moabites and decided to send for me. He saw that his forces were greatly outnumbered and would be unable to resist an invasion by the travelling masses.

His messengers told me that king Balak was worried that the Israelites would attack, defeat his army and destroy his people completely. He had sent them with money in order to persuade me to put a curse on the Israelites so that, in the event of a battle, the Moabites, assisted by the Midianites, would triumph. It was not as easy as that! My words on their own were worth nothing, the Lord's will was what mattered!

I told the messengers to spend the night at my place while I consulted the Lord. When He spoke to me, the Lord told me not to go with the messengers and that I must not curse the people of Israel because they had His blessing! First thing in the morning, I told king Balak's

41

envoy to return to Moab and to tell the king that I could not accept his payment, as the Lord had told me not to curse the Israelites.

The king was more anxious than ever when he heard of my response and in a state of mind approaching panic, he sent a larger group of much more important men to beg me to come to him and curse "these people". They promised me that I would be richly rewarded if I did. Putting the temptation of wealth behind me, I informed them that the will of God had to be obeyed and that all the gold and silver in the palace would not persuade me otherwise. As a concession, however, I suggested that they stayed the night to allow me to consult, once again, with the Lord.

On this occasion, God told me to get ready to go with the men but that I must do only what He told me. Now He had not said that I should go, only that I should get ready to go, but the thought of the rich reward caused me to pre-empt God's instruction. I got ready, as God had told me but then I went with the men from Moab. Quite unaware that I had overstepped the mark, I rode on my old, faithful donkey with two of my servants alongside.

Suddenly, the donkey turned off the road into a field. "What on earth is this animal up to?" I thought. No matter how hard I tried, it would not be guided back on to the road. Finally, in a temper, I beat the animal with a stick and forced it to return to the road. We carried on without incident until we came to a point where the road passed between two vineyards. Walls on either side caused the road to narrow and, unaccountably, my donkey squeezed against the side of one of the walls crushing my foot! "What a stupid, stupid animal!", I cried. Again, I beat it and our journey continued. Just a little further on, the road narrowed even more and, unbelievably, my donkey came to a halt and laid down! That was too much! I jumped up and started beating it for a third time. The donkey looked round at me and spoke! Yes! The donkey! Was it a dream? If not, it had to be the work of God! It asked me why I had beaten it three times. Still angry, I told it that it deserved to be killed for its behaviour. Then I thought,

42

"Am I really having a conversation with a donkey?" but it replied that it had served me faithfully all my life and asked if I had even considered that there might have been a reason for its actions. I knew it had a point! Just then, God opened my eyes and revealed an angel standing there with a sword in his hand. I realised that the donkey must have seen the angel on those three occasions causing it to take the action it had. The angel chastised me, firstly for beating the donkey and then, for undertaking the journey ahead of God's command. He confirmed that he had barred the way on those three occasions and that the donkey's action had saved me from Divine punishment! It was, of course, all true!

I confessed my sin and offered to go back home leaving the Moabites to go on their way but I was directed to go with them and cautioned to speak only the words God would give me. King Balak was relieved and delighted to see me but I warned him that I would only say what God told me to.

On three separate occasions, king Balak made an offering to God but each time the Lord would only allow the Israelites to be blessed, not cursed. Eventually, king Balak in frustration, told me that I should go home without the reward as I had not delivered the curse he had requested. I replied that God's word had been proclaimed and I prophesied that sometime in the future the people of Israel would conquer all his territories.

Then I went home having, well and truly, learned the lesson from a donkey that God's word must not be changed or adapted to suit a personal preference

JOSHUA

"Be determined and confident for the Lord your God is with you" was the word from God throughout my life and I am glad I took it to heart, for it stood me in good stead on many occasions.

When we Israelites left the slavery in Egypt behind and were led by Moses through the wilderness we saw God's great power in action and I knew my faith in Him was not misplaced.

Moses chose me, Joshua, to be his helper and during the time we spent in the wilderness I often accompanied him when he went into the innermost part of the tabernacle and to Mount Sinai where Moses spoke to the Lord face to face. In addition, when we were attacked by the Amalekites, I was chosen to lead our people in the battle, where, as long as Moses held up his hands over the battle field we gained ascendency. We won a complete victory that day because Aaron and Hur held his hands up.

Then came the day when the Lord told us to take possession of the country He had promised to our ancestors Abraham, Isaac and Jacob. Moses chose twelve men, one from each tribe, to check out the lay of the land. Ten of the twelve reported that the inhabitants were so big and powerful that we would be easily repelled. Caleb and I had faith that God would give us victory, but the opinion of the majority held sway. As a result God said that we were to wander in the wilderness for forty years and that no one of our generation, except Caleb and I, would be permitted to enter this promised land - and so it proved!

During this time Moses was kept fully occupied by having to settle disputes which arose among the people who would form long queues waiting to present their case. This went on from morning till night, day after day until Jethro, Moses father-in-law, paid a visit to the camp. He warned Moses that he would wear himself out trying to decide the right and wrong of every disagreement and suggested that he appoint men called judges to settle matters, with only the most difficult cases being referred to Moses. The wisdom of this advice was plain to Moses and he appointed God-fearing men to act as judges in the settlement of disputes.

Towards the end of the forty years Moses was very old and the Lord told him to appoint me as his successor which he did by placing his hands on me and giving me his blessing. Eleazar the priest was to be my guide and advisor as he had been given the Urim and Thummim - a device which enabled him to know God's will. I was deeply saddened when Moses died and all our people grieved long and hard for our loss.

Then, once again the Lord spoke telling us it was time to take possession of the promised land. He told us that the people living there had become so wicked and offensive to Him that we were to destroy all of them or drive them completely out of the land.

Yet again the Lord revealed His mighty power for we had the difficult task of crossing the river Jordan which was in flood but as soon as the priests responsible for the Covenant box stepped into the river, the flow of water ceased and we were able to cross over easily. When we reached the other side the flow of water resumed and the river was in spate. Not knowing the area well we sent two men to reconnoitre. While they were in Jericho a prostitute named Rahab saved their lives by sheltering them in her home. We told her that because of her actions she would be protected when we invaded. I am glad we did for Jesus was a descendant of Rahab.

With the information gained on their spying mission we decided to attack the town. Jericho, however, was well protected by defensive walls all around but again God helped us. We were to march around the city once, for each of six days. On the seventh day we were to march around the city seven times, blow our trumpets and then shout at the top of our voices. We did as God had told us! At our shout the

45

walls of Jericho came tumbling down and we took the city killing all its inhabitants, except Rahab and her family, as God had directed. He had also instructed that no one was to take any loot but the temptation was too much for a man called Achan who kept for himself some thing of value from Jericho. As a result when we tried to take the next city of Ai, we were beaten back! The Lord revealed to us the reason for our defeat was Achan's disobedience. We stoned to death Achan and his family!

Our next attempt at seizing Ai was successful. Thereafter, we slowly took possession of more and more of the land until we had enough to share among our twelve tribes. Actually only eleven tribes shared the land as the Levites were retained in God's service for the upkeep and safeguard of the sacred artefacts of our worship and instead of land they were to be supported by the other eleven tribes. Unfortunately, we did not take all of the land nor destroy all the people and as a result there were areas where pagan gods were still worshipped and sin was prevalent. Over the years these abominations managed to infiltrate our customs and weaken our whole society so that much to God's disgust, the worship of false gods took place amongst the Israelites. When Eleazar and I died no new leader was appointed and therefore the system of judges, established by Moses, became the sole discipline of control for our people until the introduction of the monarchy with the anointing of king Saul many years later.

"Be determined and confident" He had told me and as I look back on my life, I recognise that this advice from God is the only way to exercise real faith in Him!

RAHAB

My name is Rahab and I was in what is known as the world's oldest profession - yes I was a prostitute! Perhaps it did not quite have the stigma in those days that it earned later but it certainly did not put me in the upper class of society.

The whole town of Jericho, where I lived, had heard of the amazing events surrounding the people called the Hebrews or Israelites and how their God had worked so many wondrous miracles in freeing them from Egyptian slavery and protecting them as they wandered through the wilderness.

We had, therefore, a great deal of trepidation when we learned that their whole troupe was camped just beyond the river Jordan and, rumour had it, that they were planning to attack our town! With a God like that in their favour, what chance would we have of survival? I felt instinctively that this was a God I wanted to serve and worship, and when I discovered two foreigners in our town I suspected they might be Israelite spies and so I offered to hide them in my house that night.

The king of Jericho had heard that spies had come to me and sent soldiers to investigate. When I was questioned, I misdirected the king's men and sent them off on a false trail. Later the Israelite men were able to return to their camp promising that my family and I would not be harmed when the invasion took place. The signal which would protect me from being attacked by their army was a red cord which I was to tie to my window.

There was no sign of them for several days because, as I learned later, God had commanded Joshua that the mark of the covenant which God had originally made with their ancestor Abraham - that is

47

circumcision – and which had been discontinued during the wilderness journey had now to be reinstated. Joshua ordered this rite to be carried out on all the uncircumcised males and they remained in their camp at Gilgal until they recovered from the tenderness.

A little later we saw them! Thousands of men, ready for battle, and they proceeded to do a very strange thing. They marched round the city walls - just once - and then went back to camp! I immediately tied the red cord to my window as had been arranged. They repeated this manoeuvre the following day, and the next! In fact they did it for six consecutive days. However, on the seventh day something different happened! They marched round the city walls seven times and then blew their trumpets! This was followed by a loud shout which, I am sure, could have been heard from miles away! I looked, shocked, to see our proud walls crumble and the Israelites come storming into the city. The men of Jericho battled fiercely but it was obvious that God was on the side of the attackers as they overcame and slaughtered the townsfolk with little difficulty!

I hoped and prayed to their God that the Israelite soldiers would be aware of the promise the spies had made to me. Thankfully, they were and I was relieved that my family and I were allowed to go free - the only survivors of the Israelite onslaught! I made sure that my children always worshipped the God of our conquerors and, indeed, one of my descendant, a man called Boaz, inherited that faith. He was a fair-minded, hard working man who became wealthy and I was delighted when he married a Moabite girl named Ruth for through them I was blessed to become the ancestor of many Israelite kings and even of the Saviour of the world himself! Hard to believe isn't it? That someone like me, a prostitute, should be listed alongside the famous patriarchs of God's chosen people as an ancestor of Jesus Christ! It tells me that, no matter what we have done, if we are prepared to respond to the urging of God, there is hope!

The ways of God never failed to amaze me, from the miracles I had only heard about to those I witnessed personally. Sometimes I wonder what would have happened if I had not helped the Israelite spies. I, and my family, would probably have been killed and Boaz would not have been alive to produce descendants like David, Solomon and Jesus. But these are foolish conjectures, for if something is in God's plan He will not fail to bring it about! I think it is true to say that we can be thankful, therefore, that He is concerned for everyone of us and wants only what is best for us!

DEBORAH

For years after Joshua died and the Israelites had taken possession of the promised land, they, initially, remained faithful to the Lord God but the remnants of the Canaanites were never eliminated and as time passed their foreign ways crept into our culture to such an extent that many of our people began worship the gods Baal and Astartes instead of the Lord. As this happened, so we placed ourselves outside of the protective influence of our God and became vulnerable to attacks by the Canaanites. We had, therefore, lost much of our security and often lived in a state of tension, fearful, and not knowing when our towns would be invaded and their inhabitants killed by our enemies.

It was at such a time that I, Deborah, became one of the very few women judges ever to be appointed in Israelite history. Our land had fallen under control of Jabin, king of the Canaanite city of Hazor and we were being cruelly oppressed.

One day the Lord commanded me to instruct Barak, a fellow Israelite, to assemble an army which would be used to restore our independence. Barak agreed but only on condition that I went with him. The Lord's message to him then, was that he would achieve victory but it would be a woman, and not he, who would be credited with the death of Sisera, the commander of king Jabin's army.

Our troops were told to go Mount Tabor and to fight the Canaanites at the river Kishon which we did. Sisera commissioned King Jabin to send in his formidable 900 iron chariots as reinforcements for his soldiers but to no avail for Barak attacked effectively and our men were successful, slaughtering all the enemy soldiers. Sisera, however, managed to escape and took refuge in the tent of Jael, wife of Heber who had a pact of peace with king Jabin.

Jael welcomed him, gave him a drink of milk and hid him behind a curtain. After telling her to stand guard at the entrance of the tent to protect him, Sisera was so tired that he fell fast asleep. Realising that the arrival of the Israelite force was immanent, Jael felt she might be in danger from them if they discovered that she was harbouring the enemy commander and so she developed a plan to protect herself and her family. Quietly, she found a tent peg and a hammer, approached the sleeping Sisera and hammered the tent peg right through the side of his head and into the ground. It was all over so quickly that Sisera did not even utter a sound.

Shortly after, Barak and his troops arrived and started to ask questions regarding the whereabouts of Sisera. Jael said she would take them to him and led them to the spot where she had killed the man they were searching for. Sisera was still lying there with the tent peg through his head. And so it was that our victory was complete and Jael was praised for her actions!

After the battle Barak and I composed and sang a song together, praising the Lord's mighty power and commending the action of Jael in killing Sisera.

As a judge , I would often sit under a palm tree between Ramah and Bethel where the people would seek me out to settle their disputes or to seek my advice which I was happy to dispense for the Lord enabled me to decide matters fairly and I was known to be impartial in my decisions and to have the gift of wisdom from God Himself. It was also known that I was a prophetess, again, a position which was quite rare for a woman but I was pleased that the Lord thought highly enough of me to convey His will through a female like me!

All through the history of the Israelites it seems that whenever we lived for God we prospered but when we turned away from Him and lived for ourselves we were overtaken by disaster. As a nation we took our eyes off God far too readily and suffered the consequences - perhaps as individuals we can learn the lesson from this.

GIDEON

Many years after Joshua had led the Israelites into the promised land and our tribes had spread all over the territory, we began to worship the gods of the original inhabitants and forsake the Lord. Even my father took care of an altar to the foreign god Baal. As a result we had foolishly neglected the privilege of communicating with the Lord in prayer and by the time I, Gideon, was a man we were being persecuted and in subjection to the Midianites, who were nomadic camel riding desert tribesmen from the east. Fierce and ruthless they, in conjunction with the Amalekites, would invade, take what they wanted and move on. There were so many of them that we were helpless against them.

Often they would leave us in peace to plant our fields but at harvest time they would come, steal our crops and any sheep, cattle, and donkeys they could find leaving us with very little. It got so bad that many of us lived in caves or secret places in order to hide from them. Under that oppression some of us, in desperation, turned once again to the Lord. In response the Lord sent a prophet who reminded us of the power God had displayed in the past and told us that we had disobeyed His command not to worship other gods. Then the angel of the Lord came to Ophrah where I lived and spoke to me directly telling me that God was with me. I complained that the Lord seemed to have abandoned us but even as the words were being spoken I knew that it was really we who had abandoned Him. I was told that I had been chosen to deliver Israel from the Midianites and that I should tear down the altar to Baal. I did destroy Baal's altar and the symbol of the goddess Asherah which was alongside it. The whole neighbourhood wanted to kill me for so doing but my father defended me and said that if Baal was a real God he would take revenge himself.

Then I felt the Spirit move me - some might say I had a sudden rush of blood to the head - but I sent messengers throughout the land calling men to join the fight against our oppressors. Around 30,000 men responded but I started to have doubts. The combined force of Midianites and Amalekites numbered in the region of 130,000. Had I just imagined God's message to me? I had to be sure before I could risk the slaughter of so many of my compatriots. I asked God to give me a sign - that some wool which I placed on the ground would be wet in the morning while the ground around it would be dry. Next morning I rushed to see and it was as I had requested. A sure sign? However, the doubts arose again. Of course, the wool could have absorbed and held the dew which may have evaporated from the land. So tentatively I asked the Lord to make the wool dry and the land wet next morning. Again it was just as I had asked. No more doubts then!

Where would I get more men? I asked the Lord. I could hardly believe what He told me - we had too many men - I was to send home those whose hearts were not in the battle! Over 20,000 left. How were we supposed to gain a victory with only about 10,000 men? I asked the Lord. again I could hardly believe what He said - we still had too many! The Lord showed me how to select the ones He wanted. We were left with 300! I didn't ask the Lord any more - just in case! However, He told me that He wanted to show His mighty power and defeat an army of 130,000 with just 300 men so that we Israelites could not claim the victory was our own doing!

Well, He was the Almighty and against a vast army I reasoned that if our 300 had God on our side, we had more resources than they had! We attacked at night! Each of us had a trumpet and jars. We split into three groups and as we were about to attack we blew our trumpets, smashed the jars then shouted at the top of our voices. The opposing army must have thought they were faced with an enormous a number of enemy soldiers and panicked. In the dark, and in their confusion, they started to attack each other while running away. Our other men, those who had been given permission to leave, saw the disarray and decided to join us in the battle. It was bloody!! Some 120,000 of the desert tribesmen were slaughtered.

When it was all over the people of Israel wanted me to be their ruler. I declined but requested that I be given the earrings belonging to the dead. When I weighed my gift it amounted to 20 kilograms. From the earrings, I made what I intended to be a memorial of our victory but I am afraid it became more of an idol! However, the Lord allowed us to live in peace for 40 years after that.

I never forgot the lesson that, even against impossible odds, if God is fighting our battle then we are on the winning side!!

JEPHTHAH

When I think of what I did the words rash, foolhardy, imprudent, reckless and unthinking come readily to mind but there is another word which describes how I felt as a result of my action - distraught! But let me start at the beginning.

Years after Gideon died, the Israelites once again stopped worshipping the Lord and turned to foreign gods. In fact, they honoured just about any alternative to the one true God, with the result that the Lord allowed them to be overrun by the Philistines and the Ammonites, who oppressed them for eighteen years. When things became unbearable the Israelites remembered the Lord, turned back to Him, confessed their sins and pleaded for His help. The Almighty reminded them that in the past He had given them victory after victory over the very people who were now persecuting them and yet they had chosen to abandon Him in order to worship the gods of the countries they had previously defeated. "Why do these gods not help you now?" He asked. Realising their foolishness the people of Israel tore down the shrines to the foreign gods and once again worshipped the Lord.

As He saw their distress, the Lord listened to His people once more. However, the Ammonite army was camped in Gilead preparing for battle and the heads of the twelve Israelite tribes assembled in Mizpah to try to select someone who would be able to lead them in battle, and that's where I came in! My name is Jephthah and I was respected as a strong leader having distinguished myself in battle on several occasions. That respect did not extend to my own family, however. You see my mother was an unmarried prostitute and my father, Gilead, had others sons by his own wife. As a result my brothers compelled me to leave home saying that I was not entitled to any inheritance since my mother was not my father's wife.

I was forced to flee to the land of Tob and it was while I was there that I was sought out by the Israelite leaders from Gilead who requested that I should lead them in the war against the Ammonites. They knew that I had been rejected by my brothers and they had done nothing to prevent it, a fact which I cast up to them! Be that as it may, they were prepared to make me their ruler if I was able to bring about victory in the battle.

We all went to Mizpah where, in the presence of the Lord, my jurisdiction over the people of Gilead was proclaimed, whereupon I sent messengers to the king of the Ammonites in an effort to settle matters peacefully but the communication developed into a mind game and conflict proved to be inevitable.

It was as I prayed to the Lord, desperately asking for victory, that my indiscretion became evident. I made a solemn promise to God that if He gave me victory over the Ammonites, I would give Him, as a burnt offering, the first person I saw coming out of my house to greet me on my return after the victory. Can you understand my logic? If we were defeated we would all, undoubtedly, be put to death. Wasn't it better that one person should die in order for us to prevail? Well anyway, the promise was made and the battle commenced! We gained the upper hand, defeating our enemy in town after town. In fact, twenty cities were conquered by our men and the Ammonite army was slaughtered.

In the heat of the battle I forgot all about the promise I had made and the thrill of success superseded all other thoughts. These things wear off however and in the end, I set off on my way back home to Mizpah. At first, I was still congratulating myself on being such a victorious leader but as I neared my home the memory of that promise started to haunt me. Who would be the first person to greet me? It would be hard to sacrifice anyone but I hoped it would not be my only child, my lovely, delightful daughter!

In the distance I saw my house. No one was outside! I drew closer knowing that someone would soon see me. The door opened and my worst fears were realised as she came running, skipping, dancing, playing the tambourine, so happy to see me - my daughter! She put her arms around me in a hug and wondered why I was weeping. "Why did it have to be you?" I exclaimed. When I explained about the promise I had made to the Sovereign Lord she simply said that if I had made a solemn promise to God I had to keep it!

She asked to be given two months in which to grieve with her friends and when I agreed she went off to the mountains with several companions. Part of me was hoping she would not come back but at the end of the two months, there she was! I kept my promise and she died - still a virgin!

The Lord allowed me to be victorious in battle again and I remained the leader of the Israelites for six years but all that time - yes; I felt distraught as I blamed myself for making such a headstrong and perhaps, unnecessary promise in the heat of the moment - how injudicious it can be to speak without considering the consequences!!

SAMSON

When people talk about me they often say that Samson was perhaps the strongest man who ever lived but they usually fail to mention the strength of my passions which strength was, paradoxically, my weakness.

I was born of the tribe of Dan and was dedicated as a Nazirite at birth. Now a Nazirite is someone who is dedicated to the Lord for a period of special service during which time he is expected to follow certain rules such as: not cutting his hair, and not touching dead bodies etc. That time period could be fairly short or lengthy - in my case it was for life and the particular blessing through which God chose to work in me was unnatural physical strength.

I was a leader in Israel for 20 years although the country was under Philistine control at the time. When I fell in love with a Philistine girl, a marriage was arranged but during the week long celebration some underhand trickery was played on me by the Philistines and by my wife who was then given to the man who had been the best man at the wedding feast. You can imagine how angry I was and so I caught 300 foxes, tied them together in pairs by the tail and put a torch in each of the knots. I destroyed their corn fields and the previously harvested corn by setting the foxes loose thereby, burning all the crops. The Philistines put my wife to death and burned down the house of her father. Fury erupted in me and I killed several of them.

Several men from Judah were sent to arrest me and I allowed them to tie me up. When we arrived in Lehi, hordes of Philistines came running towards me bent on doing me harm. I felt the power of God pulse through my body and broke the ropes with which I had been bound. The jaw-bone of an ass which had died recently was lying nearby. I picked it up and used it as a weapon. God's power was unleashed on them and anyone who came within reach was killed. As I walked away I saw that there were about 1000 dead or dying Philistines lying on the ground. What's more I didn't feel bad about it! It felt as if the awesome might of God's power had gone into battle against sin!!

Then my passion found a new outlet in the form of a woman named Delilah! She was so attractive and seductive that I was entranced by her. But unknown to me the five Philistine kings had offered her a large sum of money to find the secret of my strength. She pestered me so much that I gave her different, but false, explanations. Each time I did, she tested them out and the Philistines were called to attack me but because the answers were incorrect, my strength did not leave me and I beat them off easily.

Finally she nagged so much that I told her the truth - that as part of the Nazirite covenant my hair had never been cut and if it were to be, my special blessing of great strength would be at an end. Yes!! I know! It was plain stupid but sometimes when your emotions are involved common sense gets thrown out the window.

Next morning I was awakened from sleep to find Philistine soldiers all around me and thought I would chase them as usual but my arms and legs felt weak. I couldn't believe I had so little strength. Then I realised that Delilah must have told the Philistines and my hair had been shorn. They easily overpowered me, took me prisoner and put out my eyes!!

When the pain of that subsided I was set to work grinding grain in the prison feeling helpless, thinking day after day of the way in which Delilah had betrayed me. But my hair was growing again!

Sometime later the five Philistine kings held a celebration to their god Dagon and thought they would have some fun at my expense. I was led into the centre of the temple court and could hear the derisory, mocking of the crowd. "Is this supposed to be the mighty Samson? Where is his strength now?" were just some of the jeers with which they teased me! I told the lad who was leading me to let my hands rest on the pillars which supported the building. Their gloating grew louder as they shouted praise to their god. I prayed to the Lord and at once could feel the old strength flood my body. They started to laugh as I pushed against the pillars "Poor blind fool" they said. Then, silence started to spread through the crowd as they felt the building tremble. They stood, shocked as more and more power flowed through my body till eventually the pillars gave way and thousands of them died as the building collapsed.

It has been said that I killed more Philistines at my death than I ever did during my life. May the Lord be praised.

RUTH

Hi folks - I'm Ruth. I lived at a time before there were kings in Israel and although I'm not an Israelite by birth I am by marriage - twice! I was living in Moab when I married my first husband who was a fine man named Mahlon and my mother in law, Naomi, who originally came from Bethlehem, was a real gem - you'll get no mother in law jokes from me! Noami had come to Moab with her husband, Elimelech because there had been a severe famine in Israel.

Things went well for a while but then Naomi's husband died suddenly and, sadly, about ten years later, my husband died also as did Naomi's other son. It was a terrible time for Naomi and me and my sister in law Orpah but we had a very strong bond of love which helped us through.

With no real means of support Naomi decided to go back to her home land. We two girls wanted to go with her but Naomi felt it might be better if we returned to our own families. After some pleading and tears Orpah left but I just couldn't leave Naomi and begged her to let me go with her. I guess I must have worn her down because she eventually agreed. Really, I think she was pleased because I know she loved me too.

When we arrived in Bethlehem it took a little time to get used to the customs of the people in this land which was new to me but with the help of Naomi it all quickly fell into place. Naomi's old friends recognised her and welcomed her warmly. It was plain to see that she was well respected by her own people. I was able to harvest some corn from the sides of the fields for it was the custom in those days that strangers and foreigners could pick crops from the edges of the fields which the farmers left unharvested for that very purpose. It was backbreaking work but it meant we could at least have something to eat. Then I saw him!! The owner of the field!! A man called Boaz. He was special - but of course I couldn't let him see that my hands were shaking - my heart was beating faster too - Oh! I hoped he wasn't married! I've never believed in love at first sight but there was certainly some chemistry at work. When he saw me picking the leftover grain he ordered his men not to molest me and to deliberately leave large bundles of corn for me to pick up.

When I took the pickings back to Naomi she was surprised and when I told her what Boaz had done she was delighted - she knew that Boaz was a kinsman-redeemer; that is a relative of hers who perhaps had the right and duty to ask me to marry him. That pleased and excited me. Naomi told me to go to his place one night and as I trusted Naomi's judgement, I did.

When Boaz discovered me there I told him how I felt about him and watched his face anxiously for a sign that would convey his feelings. What I saw there told me that he felt the same way. Soon, we were discussing the possibility of marriage and were both very much in favour of the idea - but apparently we had one big problem. There was another man who was a closer relative of Naomi and therefore under the Jewish custom had the first right to take me in marriage. Boaz met with this man and discussed the situation. He was magnificent and in the end persuaded the man that it was not in his best interest to marry me.

With the road opened up Boaz and I were married and you should have seen the joy on Naomi's face - she was as ecstatic as I was.

We lived happily together and now as I look back I am filled with pride and joy and gratitude to God for the way He unveiled His will, for I was privileged to become the great grandmother of King David and the great great grandmother of King Solomon. But more than any of these is the knowledge of the blessing of God in choosing my family to be the forebears of the King of Kings, the son of God -

none other than Jesus the Christ!!! To God be the Glory! Praise His Name for ever

JOB

Men and women often use the expression "the patience of Job", but I don't know that the word 'patience' really describes what I exhibited. To tell the truth, bewildered resignation to unjustified calamity comes closer to defining the way I felt. I mean, how would you have felt if you had lost everything like I did? I was a wealthy man, happily married with seven sons and three daughters, huge numbers of camels, sheep, oxen and donkeys and with servants galore. Always, I honoured God, worshipped him and never wandered from His revealed path. I praised His name daily and offered sacrifices frequently thanking Him for my riches.

How precarious these riches were! For the day came when my world collapsed around me as I was hit by one tragedy after another. Firstly, I was informed that a raiding party of Sabeans from the south had attacked and stolen my oxen and donkeys and killed the servants who were engaged in ploughing my fields. Next, a lightning bolt struck and killed my sheep and the shepherds. Then, three bands of Chaldeans, raiders from the north, took all the camels and killed the men responsible for them. Finally, a storm blew down the house of my eldest son, killing all my children. My children gone! - servants, animals, riches all gone!! What a vacuum existed in my life then! I tried to fill it with the Lord but he just did not seem to be there for me. I tore my clothes in grief and shaved my head in my distress.

It was impossible to understand why this had happened but in prayer, I acknowledged that I came into the world with nothing and I would have nothing when I left it. God had blessed me greatly but now He had allowed me to be cursed by grief and despair. He was in control, He knew what He was doing but I wished He would let me understand. As if what had happened wasn't bad enough, I started to develop sores and in no time at all suppurating sores covered my whole body. I sat by the refuse heap scraping these sores with a piece of broken glass. The physical pain coupled with mental anguish left me a sorry sight indeed!

My wife was surprised that my faith in God was as strong as ever for she was angry with Him. I didn't overlook the fact that she was suffering great distress also but we found little comfort in shared sorrow for the pain was too deep. She suggested that I ought to curse God for having let this happen but I tried to explain how good God had been before, and if He was sending us trials now we could hardly complain. I am not sure she was entirely convinced! I am not even sure I convinced myself!

I was visited by three friends; Eliphas, Bildad and Zophar who had heard of my suffering and had come to try to comfort me. At first, they did not recognise me such was my condition but when they did they wept and tore their clothes as they identified with my pain. They said nothing, but simply sat with me in silence for seven days realising what I was going through. In the end I broke the silence by expressing my dark gloom and lamenting that I would be better off dead. They each, in turn, implied that I must have sinned for God to allow this catastrophe to occur and that I should repent and seek forgiveness. Good advice, normally, but I had already examined my life looking for sin and knew that I was blameless. We ended up almost arguing about the matter and then a younger colleague named Elihu joined the conversation. He was angry with me, because I had tried to justify myself, and with the others because they could not refute my proclamations of innocence. He told me to confess my sins and ask the Lord to pardon me.

Then the Lord spoke at last, scolding all of us by asking how could we hope to understand His ways or question His wisdom? I acknowledged my foolishness and God blessed me once again. Later, I learned that before these trials of mine came about the Almighty explained that He had such confidence in my steadfast faith that when Satan had challenged Him, He had agreed to allow the evil one to test me to the limit to see if I would turn away from God. Satan was well and truly put in his place and I am joyful for my part in that.

After this short time of suffering, God healed me and in time gave me another seven sons and three daughters and twice as many camels, sheep and donkeys as before. I lived in happy contentment for a further 140 years and thinking of the trials I went through, can echo the words of the woman who has just come through the agony of childbirth - that the pain is soon forgotten as a new life is experienced.

<u>HANNAH</u>

How could anyone be so cruel? It was bad enough not being able to have the child I yearned for so much but to have it cast up to me continually by Peninnah, my husband Elkanah's other wife, was more than I could bear. Day after day I had to listen to Peninnah brag about her offspring and to suffer the barbed insults which cut me to the quick. There was little I could retaliate with when she accused me of being so sinful that my inability to have a child was merely God's justice. Of course, it was not true but how I wished that God would make me fertile! I tried not to let the hurt show but in private I sobbed my heart out. Elkanah was sometimes concerned and tried to cheer me up "Hannah, don't be so sad all the time you know you have all my love." It didn't help. Although I knew he loved me, how could a man begin to understand the torment in my soul, and, anyway he had children by Peninnah.

In order to worship and offer sacrifices to the Lord we went, every year, from Ramah where we lived to Shiloh where there was a High Priest and a house of God. On one such occasion I went off by myself and started to pray. As I did I could not hold back the tears. I opened my heart and soul to the Lord and told Him how I felt and promised that if He gave me a son I would have him dedicated to serve God for the whole of his life. With tears dripping from my chin I continued in silent prayer for a long time. Although they were silent I was mouthing the words of my prayers and Eli, the High Priest saw me. Thinking it was drunken babbling he scolded me "Stop drinking and sober up." he said. How could he think that of me? I let him see that I was absolutely sober and told him of my distress and that I had been praying so hard because I was in misery. He realised he had misjudged the situation, acknowledged my plight and blessed me saying "May God grant your request". My spirits were lifted and I felt an unusual confidence that God had listened to my prayer.

We returned to Ramah next day and my baby was conceived that very night. When he was born I named him Samuel which in Hebrew indicates that I had asked for him in the name of the Lord. My joy was boundless - no more would I have to suffer the scorn and humiliation from Peninnah. I felt my life was fulfilled but I knew I had to keep my promise and let my son serve in the house of God. The time came for our annual trip to Shiloh but I said to Elkanah that I would prefer to stay home on this occasion so that Samuel could be weaned. I also told him of my promise that Samuel would be dedicated to God after he was weaned. He understood and agreed.

For the few short years I had Samuel with me I was in rapture - my own son - what a delight but I dreaded the time when he was to be given up to the service of God. Of course, time passes so quickly and all too soon he was old enough to be taken to God's house in Shiloh where he was given to Eli as I had promised. A mixture of pride, joy, sadness and loneliness flooded my mind! I thanked the Lord for giving him to me but how hard it was to part with him! He was still too young to realise what was happening but I hoped he would understand, as he grew up, just how much he was loved - and missed!

Every year I channelled all the energy of love for my absent son into making him a beautiful little coat and he was always happy to receive this present from his mother. Each time I saw him I could see he was being well looked after because he was growing up to be a fine boy. I looked forward to each of these visits with ecstasy. I know he did too and it became quite clear that he loved serving the Lord. Always, I came away from Shiloh feeling happy and sad at the same time. I comforted myself with the thought that at least Peninnah could not brag about her children because my child was in God's service which carried the greatest prestige.

Eli again blessed me through Elkanah saying "May the Lord give you other children to replace the one you dedicated to him". The Lord did! I had three more sons and two daughters while Samuel grew to serve God in a mighty way.

He was always in my prayers and I never failed to thank God for the wonderful way He answered those prayers

ELI

The sacred Covenant Box, built during the days of Moses, was kept in the house of the Lord in Shiloh. This was the town in which Joshua had established the tabernacle, and so it had become the centre of worship for the whole of Israel. I, Eli, a Levite, was serving as High Priest and my two sons, Hophni and Phinehas, were also priests. I wish I could say I was proud of them but they were selfish and self-centred and they treated the animal offerings made by the worshippers with complete disrespect taking the best parts for themselves. I had told them again and again that they must observe the regulations handed down through the generations but they ignored my instructions.

At that time a woman named Hannah dedicated her son, Samuel, to the Lord's service and I took care of him, teaching him the ways of the Lord. He responded in a far better way than Hophni and Phinehas had ever done and I began to wish that he had been my son. On one occasion, when he was just a boy, he came to me in the middle of the night and asked why I had called him. I hadn't called him so I sent him back to bed. As this happened three times in a brief period, I realised that it was the voice of God he had heard. He had been sleeping in the area of the Covenant Box where God had spoken to our great leaders in the past and so I told him that if he heard the voice again to say "Speak Lord, Your servant is listening".

Next morning I enquired if he had been given a message from God. He seemed reluctant to tell me but I persisted until he did. Perhaps it would have been better for me not to know. The word of God was that the members of my family were to be punished and that something terrible was to happen to Israel. It confirmed the words of a prophet who had previously told me that my sons would die on the same day and that my whole clan would suffer because I had failed to prevent my sons from dishonouring the Lord.

Samuel continued to grow and it became obvious that the Lord was with him. The messages he proclaimed all came to pass and he was respected as a prophet by people all over the land.

Then came the day when God carried out His threat! The Philistines attacked Israel and 4,000 Israelites were killed and the remainder forced to retreat. Our men believed that if the Covenant Box were to be brought to the battle zone then God would give us victory. They were unaware of the message young Samuel had confided in me.

The Covenant Box was duly taken to our troops but we were soundly beaten and the Covenant Box captured. I was an old man by that time and when I learned that my two sons had been killed in the battle and that the Covenant Box had been captured, the shock caused me to fall breaking my neck. I died there, having been a ruler and Judge in Israel for forty years.

Grief at the defeat and the loss of the treasured Covenant Box was widespread from one end of Israel to the other. However capturing our precious symbol of God's presence was not the great triumph the Philistines had hoped it would be, for the Lord caused tumours to afflict the Philistine people the whole time they possessed it. Eventually, they understood that it was the presence of the Covenant Box which was causing their problems and they sent it back to us with gifts which, they hoped, would appease our God.

It arrived at Beth Shemesh in our territory where the people celebrated greatly but some of them became daring and opened it to look inside, something which was forbidden to them! Those who did died immediately! The inhabitants of Beth Shemesh became afraid that they might inadvertently do something else which would offend God so they sent a message to the townsfolk of Kiriath Jearim who took the Covenant Box back to their town where it remained for twenty years.

Samuel lived his life under God's guidance and when the Philistines attacked once again, the Lord gave Samuel a resounding victory. While he lived the Philistines were never again successful in attacking Israel. I was pleased that Samuel became a mighty man of God and hope my influence contributed, to some degree, in that regard but in comparison to him I realise I was, perhaps, just too casual in my service to God. Hopefully others will reap the benefit of my hindsight!

SAMUEL

Although I was not involved in making the decision I am glad my mother dedicated me to the service of God as a child because the thrill of hearing the Lord speak directly to me was beyond words. I remember the first time it happened. I was just a young boy when I heard a voice calling my name in the middle of the night. I believed it to be my master Eli but when I went to him he told me to go back to bed. When this happened three times Eli realised that it was the Lord who was calling me and so he told me that if it happened again I should say "speak Lord your servant is listening". When I did, the Lord gave me a message but it did not auger well for my mentor, Eli, whose family had offended God and were to suffer the Lord's punishment.

As I grew to manhood I continued to convey God's word and the people throughout the land recognised me as a prophet, ruler and judge. Yes, I was held in high regard but my sons failed to win the confidence of the Israelites and as I grew old I could hear the grumbles "We trust Samuel but do not want his sons to lead us". Eventually it became quite clear that they wanted to be ruled by an appointed king, as other countries were, rather than by my children. God spoke to me again telling me to let them have their king and indicated the man He had selected to serve in that position. The future king was from the tribe of Benjamin. His name was Saul, son of Kish, and he lived in Gibeah.

When we first met I thought he looked the part and that the people would look up to him and not only because he was so tall but he had the bearing fit for a royal throne. I explained to him privately that God had chosen him to rule the people of Israel and anointed him with olive oil. The whole country was called to a religious meeting at Mizpah where I officially anointed Saul as king.

About one month later the Israelite city of Jabesh in Gilead was besieged by king Nahash of Ammon but the Lord gave Saul the first of his victories and the Ammonites were slaughtered. Great celebrations took place at the victory and the Israelites began to have confidence in Saul. I felt it was time to make quite clear to them the reality of the situation and so when they were once again gathered together I told them they had sinned by rejecting God as their king and asking for a human ruler but if they and their king honoured the Lord and obeyed his commands then they would gain God's favour.

Sadly, Saul began to think he was self-sufficient, as illustrated on one occasion when we were about to go to war with the Philistines. I arrived on the scene to find that Saul had become impatient awaiting my arrival and had offered a sacrifice to the Lord himself. He was not a priest and was not permitted to do such a thing but instead of acknowledging and repenting of his action he tried to justify himself. God decided that his time as king was to be curtailed and another, more worthy, man would take his place!

However with the help of his son, Jonathan, Saul defeated the Philistines and won an heroic reputation with great victories over his other enemies. Perhaps, I thought, God was giving him a second chance. If that was the case Saul failed again! I informed him the Lord had decreed that the wickedness of the Amalekites should be punished and that he was to attack and destroy everything connected with them. Saul did successfully attack and destroyed almost everything but under pressure from his troops he decided to keep the best of the animals to offer as a sacrifice to the Lord. Saul again tried to justify himself when I told him that his behaviour was rebellious. How could he think of offering as a sacrifice to the Lord something which had been tainted with the sins of the Amalekites? He also allowed the wicked Philistine king, Agag, to live. God made it clear that He preferred obedience rather than offerings and sacrifice. Then

Saul acknowledged his sin but it was too late because God had rejected him as king. I had king Agag brought before me and personally executed this evil man thereby carrying out the task that God had entrusted to Saul. Then I went home to Ramah and Saul to Gibeah. I never saw Saul again!

The whole incident made me very sad but the Lord spoke again telling me to go to Bethlehem to anoint the man He had chosen to replace Saul as king of Israel. I was directed to invite a man called Jesse and his family to participate in a sacrifice. Seven of Jesse's sons appeared one by one but the Lord declared that none of them was the one He had chosen. When asked if he had another son, Jesse replied that the youngest was taking care of the sheep. I delayed the sacrifice until he arrived. He was a fine young man and the Lord told me that he was the one. Right there and then, I anointed David, Jesse's eighth son, with olive oil. Immediately a change came over the young lad as the Spirit of the Lord took control of his life. Saul, on the other hand, had forsaken God's Spirit and was afflicted by evil forces.

Unfortunately, I did not live to see David ascend to the throne but knew that whenever he did he would make an outstanding king.

DAVID

To say I was surprised would be an understatement of gigantic proportions. I had been on the hills tending the sheep when I heard a call: "David! David! - the prophet Samuel is at your house and he wants to see you!" Me? Why me? The great prophet Samuel wanted me? What had I done? I hurried home and - yes, it was true - the great man of God was there. Surprise turned to amazement when he told me that I had been chosen to be the future king of Israel. He anointed me with olive oil and I was aware of a glow inside making me feel clean and eager to serve the Lord my God. However, while Saul was on the throne I would continue to be his willing subject.

I was sad to learn that Saul was having severe mood swings caused by the influence of an evil spirit but whenever soothing music was played it eased his condition. Apparently he had heard of my ability on the harp and enlisted me into his service. Saul approved of me and I became his personal weapons carrier. During my time in that position the Philistines gathered to attack us yet again. On this occasion, their champion, a man called Goliath, threw down a challenge to our army. He offered to fight any one of our soldiers in order to decide the outcome of the confrontation. Our enemies thought they were assured of victory because Goliath was a monster of a man standing about three metres tall and was built in proportion. He was a fearsome sight and none of our soldiers had any enthusiasm for the contest. For forty days Goliath bated us with his challenge which no one accepted.

When I went to the battle lines and heard this arrogant ogre scornfully invite any man to combat, I said to Saul that I would fight the giant. After a little resistance he decided to allow me to accept the challenge but I discarded all the armour I was given because it was far too cumbersome. Instead I took my sling and selected five smooth stones from a stream because I knew God was with me. You may well ask that if I was so confident in God's power why did I take five stones and not just one. Well, I felt that although God is all powerful, He was working through this imperfect servant. So, just in case the first sling shot was inaccurate, I would have others in reserve.

Goliath seeing that his opponent was just a boy, laughed contemptuously and cursed me. I replied by saying that he was coming against me with all his armour and weaponry but I came against him in the name of Almighty God. As he marched purposefully towards me I ran towards him loading one of the stones in my sling. As soon as he was within range, I let fly with a shot which hit him in the middle of the forehead. He fell to the ground with a broken skull! I ran to where he lay and used his sword to decapitate him. With their champion dead, our enemies panicked and our army routed them.

Saul was thrilled at the victory and commissioned me to be an officer in his army. In the many campaigns I led we achieved victory after victory and I became famous among the ordinary people. This made Saul jealous and feel threaten! Several times he tried to kill me but God was with me and I escaped. Although he seemed to hate me his son, Jonathan, became my best friend and his daughter Michal fell in love with me and became my wife. For the rest of his life Saul had days when he stalked me in an attempt to have me killed. In spite of my efforts to assure him that I would do him no harm his irrational behaviour caused him to persecute me indiscriminately. Eventually Saul and his three sons, including Jonathan, were killed in a later battle against the Philistines but not before he had incurred God's further wrath by consulting a spiritualist at Endor.

You might think I would be happy that my tribulations were over but, in truth, I regretted his death and grieved over the loss of my loving friend, Jonathan. With the help of Abner, the commander of

Saul's army, I became king of Israel. More victories in battle brought the combined states of Israel and Judah under my rule and I delivered the Covenant Box to Jerusalem which I established as my city.

There were times of deep regrets and pain, none more so than when my son Absolom killed his brother Amnon and attempted to wrest the monarchy from me. His rebellion caused many deaths and put my life in danger but I still loved him and when he was killed my mourning was intense.

There were also times of shame! My personal low point must have been when, before we were married and Bathsheba was married to one of my soldiers, I saw her bathing and was filled with lust. I seduced her, wanted to possess her and arranged for her husband to be killed in battle. It took a courageous prophet named Nathan to point out how wicked I had been and although I repented, the subsequent early death of the first son Bathsheba bore was God's corrective punishment. Later we had another son who one day would become my successor as king. His name was Solomon.

Thankfully there were wise people who consoled me, helped me, advised me and corrected me during the times when life was difficult but rather than wallowing in my woes I always preferred to let my mind dwell on the many, many good things God did for me for when I gave Him the honour my spirit sang!

NATHAN

It's not always easy being a prophet, in fact, sometimes it can be downright life-threatening. There are some who believe our purpose is to foretell the future but in truth that is only a small part of it. Our real objective is to declare God's will and proclaim His word and it was with such a commission that king David had to be confronted.

It was not a task I relished but who was I to question a directive from God. You see I, Nathan, had a great deal of respect for God's chosen ruler and I believe he had for me but perhaps this message would alter all that. The story, and I know it to be true, was that one evening David happened to see a beautiful woman taking a bath. Her name was Bathsheba and he was filled with lust for her. To cut a long story short, David committed adultery with Bathsheba, the wife of one of his officers - a man named Uriah. David was besotted and when he learned that she was pregnant by him, he wanted her to be one of his wives and so arranged for Uriah to be returned to the battlefield and to be placed where the fighting was heaviest. The commanding officer of David's army, Joab, was told that he should retreat leaving Uriah to be killed.

David allowed Bathsheba to mourn for an appropriate time and then they were married and she bore him a son. It was now my task to tackle David over this wrongdoing. I did so by telling him a story of two men - one rich the other poor. The poor man had a lamb - just the one - which he tended with great care and grew to love deeply. It became just like a member of his own family. The rich man wanted to prepare a meal for a visitor but rather than kill one of his own lambs he took that of the poor man. As I told him this story David became very angry and swore that the rich man ought to be put to death for such a vile, cruel deed. "You are that man!" I exclaimed

80

and reminded him of all that the Lord had done for him and said that He would have done twice as much if David had wanted. "Instead you took poor Uriah's wife and had him killed.!" I blurted out and explained how harshly he would pay for his sin. To his credit David did not try to justify his behaviour but simply acknowledged: "I have sinned against the Lord!" It was almost as if he had not realised the wickedness of his actions before. As a punishment the child that Bathsheba had borne him became ill and died a week later. During that time David refused to eat and spent his time in prayer.

He learned a lesson the hard way and, I suppose, became a better man as a result. He comforted Bathsheba and they had another son who was named Solomon which means "Peaceful" indicating they had made peace with the Lord. I was told by God that the boy should also be referred to as Jedidiah which in Hebrew signifies 'Loved by the Lord' - and so he turned out to be, for the Lord said that David's successor as king would be this son.

On another occasion David had been considering building a temple for the Lord and was eager to proceed and I was given the message that a temple would indeed be built but because of the number of people David had killed in battle, it would be his son Solomon, when he became king, who would build it and not David himself. However that prophecy came under attack when David was very old. Adonijah, one of his other sons tried to declare himself king but Bathsheba and I worked together and got David to declare Solomon king in accordance with the Lord's will. Together with Zadok, who was another priest, I anointed Solomon king at Gihon.

David had ruled the whole of Israel for 40 years when he died. He always had the Lord's purposes at heart and although human failings punctuated his life he loved the Lord and was greatly loved in return.

David would often sit and meditate on the wonder of God and he composed many poems and songs in praise of His greatness. I could appreciate that for I found, when things were at their most difficult, focusing all my attention on the loving Lord neutralized negative thoughts and gave me the courage, strength and confidence to work for the fulfilment of His purpose.

SOLOMON

"Beauty is in the eye of the beholder" they say, so perhaps wisdom is in the ear of the listener! The more it is appreciated and assimilated into our lives the greater its benefits and that applies to me as much as anyone for although it has been said that Solomon was the wisest man who ever lived, I was foolish enough to allow the sweet music of arrogance to deafen me to the still small voice of God.

My father, king David, did not live long after he appointed me king in succession to him but I well remember the blessing he gave me just before his death:- "Be determined and confident and obey all the laws given by God." This instruction became my code for living, at least for most of my life!

At the start of my reign, the most respected place of worship was at Gibeon and it was while I had gone there to worship at the tabernacle that God spoke to me in a dream. He asked me what I would like Him to give me! Realising that I was very young and that it would require great judgement to rule over the mighty nation of God's people, I asked for the wisdom to rule with justice and to see clearly the difference between good and evil. The Lord was pleased that I had not asked for wealth, fame or a long life and promised to endow me with the requested wisdom, but in addition would bestow upon me the wealth, fame and long life I had not asked for. When I returned to Jerusalem I, joyfully, made offerings to the Lord in front of the sacred Covenant Box.

One day, I had to settle a dispute between two women, each of whom claimed to be the mother of a baby boy and each demanded custody of the child. There was no evidence to indicate which of the two was telling the truth so I called for a sword and ordered that the child be cut in two and that each woman be given a half. One of the women was quite happy with that decision but the other begged me not to kill the boy and said that the other woman could have him just as long as he was allowed to live. It was then obvious which of the two was the real mother so I gave the child to the woman who had begged for his life to be spared. When the people of Israel heard of this, they seemed to develop a deep respect for my skill in passing judgement.

Under my rule the country prospered. I married an Egyptian princess and there was peace between Israel and Egypt. In addition, king Hiram of Tyre who had been a friend of my father continued that good relationship with me and we agreed to a peace treaty between our peoples. Indeed, when I started to build the Temple to the living God in Jerusalem, Hiram supplied all the cedar and pine wood we required.

Building the Temple took seven years but what a magnificent structure it was! Decorated with gold and with profuse carvings of plants and animals, so expertly done by our finest craftsmen that it brought gasps of admiration from anyone who saw it for the first time. It was a place fit for the presence of the Lord and He lived there while we gave Him the honour and respect He deserves.

When the Temple was complete, I had the Covenant Box placed in the inner sanctuary which was called the Holy of Holies and it was then that Jerusalem became established as the central place of worship in our country. We then set about improving the rest of the land, building a royal palace and rebuilding several of the cities in Israel. Meanwhile our fleet of ships grew larger and king Hiram's men joined with mine in sailing expeditions bringing back huge amounts of gold, silver and other valuables. So my wealth increased as God had promised and my fame spread abroad.

The queen of Sheba had heard of the prosperity of Israel and she decided to pay a visit. Now Sheba was a very rich region itself but the queen was astounded at the standard of living; the beauty of the

Temple and the obvious affluence of my land! She had also heard of my reputation for wisdom and asked me many questions. She was perceptibly surprised at the ease with which I answered. We exchanged many gifts and when she left I could see that she was more than impressed with Israel.

It would be nice to end on that happy note but, unfortunately, that is when I began to think I could stretch God's laws to suit myself! I married many foreign women; something which had been expressly forbidden by God and, in fact, had 300 wives and 700 concubines! Slowly but surely the influence of their pagan religions began to filter through and, to some extent in order to please them, I allowed places of worship to foreign gods to be built and even joined in their worship myself!

God, our Lord, was angry and told me that when my son became king he would rule over only part of the land and that ten of the twelve tribes would be ruled by one of my officials! It took a little time but it turned out the way He described.

A wise man? Ah! yes; but there is none so foolish as a wise man who puts his pleasures before the word of God.

JEROBOAM

There I was, toiling away in a land-fill site on the east side of Jerusalem, when I heard that king Solomon had been asking my name. Next moment, I heard a shout, "Jeroboam, king Solomon is putting you in charge of all the workers in the territories belonging to the tribes of Manasseh and Ephraim!" This was quite a promotion, for those two tribes controlled a vast area of land to the north of Jerusalem. I felt greatly honoured. Apparently, the king had noticed how hard I had been working and this was his reward.

One day, departing from Jerusalem, I was met by the prophet Ahijah from Shiloh. These prophets sometimes do the strangest things for he took off his new robe, tore it into twelve pieces and gave ten of them to me. It was his way of telling me that the Lord was going to remove control of ten of the twelve tribes from Solomon's children and give it to me. This was the punishment God had decreed because Solomon had turned away from Him to worship foreign gods. When he discovered what the prophet had said, Solomon tried to have me killed but I escaped to Egypt where I lived until he died.

After his death Rehoboam, his son, succeeded him as king and the people of the ten northern tribes asked me to return to their area. In order to confirm himself as king of the north as well as the south, Rehoboam went to Shechem where he was confronted by a deputation who appealed to him for an easing of the burdensome taxes which had been levied upon them by his father. Rehoboam sought the opinions of his advisers. The older and wiser, agreed to the request of the delegation but the younger and more hot-headed said taxes should be increased! The tough approach was the decision Rehoboam made! Big mistake! The ten tribes, almost to a man, rebelled leaving Rehoboam the ruler of only Judah! History records that it was then the kingdom was split in two – Judah to the south and the ten tribes of Israel to the north. I was crowned king of Israel in fulfilment of Ahijah's prophecy! The Levites who were the priests, of course, continued to be responsible for worship at the Temple in Jerusalem which was in the south.

It was an awkward time because all our people, north and south, were in the habit of going to the Temple in Jerusalem to offer sacrifices to the Lord and I was fearful that when the people from the north went there they might decide their allegiance lay with king Rehoboam after all. It was quite possible that on their return, my life would be in danger and so I took matters into my own hands. Playing on the ill-will they were nursing towards the king in Jerusalem, I told them that they need no longer go to Jerusalem to worship and offer sacrifices! I had two gold bull-calves struck and declared that these were our gods. One of the idols I placed in Bethel, the other in Dan. To make matters worse I incurred God's further displeasure by choosing as priests, men who were not Levites.

The day came when the Lord showed me, well and truly, the error of my ways. It was at Bethel where, as I stood at the altar to offer a sacrifice, a prophet who had been sent by God from Judah decried the altar. He announced that one day a descendant of David, named Josiah, would kill these so called priests who served at the pagan altars and he claimed that the altar where I stood would fall apart. How dare he interrupt my celebration!! I ordered him to be seized! As I pointed at him, my arm became paralysed and the altar fell apart just as the prophet had said it would.

The wonder of the destruction of the altar was largely lost on me - my arm took all my attention - it would not move! I recognised this man as a prophet of the Lord, swallowed my pride and begged him to pray that the use of my arm might be restored! He prayed and my arm was healed. In the midst of all the commotion I felt grateful to him for giving me back the movement in my arm and invited him to come home to dine with me. He refused and stated that as he had now delivered the message God had given him he would return to Judah!

At that time my son, Abijah, fell ill and I sent my wife to Shiloh, to the home of the prophet Ahijah, who had originally prophesied that I would rule Israel, to ask if our son would get well. I told her to pretend to be someone else but the old prophet saw through the pretence and gave her the bad news that our son would die and that my family was to be cursed, for although God had chosen me, I had failed to obey His laws and had instituted the disgusting practice of idol worship. However, I couldn't lose face with my people and so continued to practise the things which God considered to be offensive. After all my arm was better!!

JONAH

When I think about it now it all seems like a dream - some parts more like like a nightmare! It started when I heard God call me, "Jonah!" He said, "I want you to go to Ninevah and warn the people there, that I am about to destroy their city because of their wicked ways!" I felt I was in a no-win situation. The chances were that if I told the people about God's warning they would just laugh at me and I would look like a fool. On the other hand, if they repented of their sins, God would probably excuse them and reprieve the city. Then they would consider me to be not only a fool but also a prophet of doom. Either way I was on a hiding to nothing. So, instead of going north to Ninevah, I went south to Joppa where I got on a ship going to Spain thinking I would be able to escape the Lord.

I should have known better for there is nowhere that the presence of the Creator of heaven and earth is absent. When we set sail the Lord caused such a violent storm to bombard us that the sailors were terrified and each prayed to his own god - to no avail! They jettisoned the cargo but the storm got worse! Then they decided to draw lots to see who was to blame for this desperate situation and, of course, I was pinpointed! I explained that I was a Hebrew, that my God was the Almighty Creator and that I was running away from Him. It looked very probable that we would all die anyway, so I told them to throw me overboard and the sea would become calm but they were reluctant to do so. Instead they tried to row the ship ashore but that proved impossible. Finally against their better judgement they agreed to do as I had said! They prayed to my God for forgiveness for causing my death and threw me over the side!

Immediately the sea became calm! The sailors were shocked, acknowledged the Lord and decided to serve Him! Were these converts to be the last lines in my life story? No! The Lord sent a huge fish which swallowed me whole and I remained in its insides for three days. I can't begin to describe the conditions of what I believed to be my disgusting death chamber! However, in the end, the fish was sick and I was coughed up on a beach!

The Lord spoke again repeating His command for me to go to Ninevah and proclaim His message. Looking like a fool in front of the people of Ninevah was a better option than spending more time in the stomach of a fish, so off I went!

Ninevah was a very large city and when I had travelled well into it I started to deliver God's message! "Repent and change your ways or else Ninevah will be destroyed in forty days!" To my surprise they believed me, accepted the message, fasted and wore sackcloth to show that they had repented. They prayed sincerely to God and put their evil ways behind them. Then what I feared might happen did happen! God decided not to destroy the city at that time after all! How did that make me look in the eyes of the men and women of the city? A false prophet? A prophet of doom? A worry monger? All three? It was my reputation which I was concerned about. At that time it didn't occur to me to consider just how mightily God had used me to bring salvation to so many people!

I sulked a little and told the Lord that I knew His loving-kindness would cause Him to pardon the city if they repented. My annoyance was obvious! I went to a hillside overlooking the city and suddenly a large plant grew up over me providing shade from the heat of the sun. It's strange but I became fond of that plant. I knew it was God's work and having that protective plant encouraged my mood to soften a bit. It was a lovely thing! However, next day it shrivelled up and died. Once again I complained to God - this time for allowing my plant to die!

He helped me to understand that just as I had shown concern for the plant and would like it to have been saved so He, in an infinitely

90

greater way, had concern for the people of Ninevah and wanted them to be saved!

I realise now that God's love and concern are so great and complex that they are difficult to understand - until we look at them simply, with minds released from the arrogance of human self-importance.

ELIJAH

I am Elijah, the prophet of God from Tishbe and I lived during the reign of king Ahab of Israel who became king 36 years after the death of king Jeroboam the first Israelite king of the divided kingdom. King Ahab delighted in flaunting the Lord's commands and encouraged idol worship, turning his people away from the true God. Much of his wickedness, however, was inspired by his wife, Jezebel. They both hated me because each time we met, I brought them the word from God which was always bad news for them.

On one occasion the Lord sent a drought throughout their land and I was despatched to tell the king that the drought would not end until the time that God would reveal through me. I went to a brook on the east side of the river Jordan where the Lord commanded ravens to bring me food.

From there I was sent to Zarephath where God told me I would be fed by a widow. On arriving at the town, I spotted a widow gathering firewood and asked her to bring me a drink of water and some bread. She was happy to get me the water but confessed that she had no bread. Her sole provisions were a handful of flour and a drop of oil, after using which, she and her son would starve. Because of the drought food was scarce everywhere. However, I knew that the Lord would provide and told her to make a loaf with what she had, for God would not allow her supplies to run out before the rains came. And so it proved!

While I was living there the widow's son became seriously ill and a few days later he died. Naturally she was beside herself with grief and blamed me because, in her mind, she felt that my presence had made God notice her sins and punish her with the death of her son. I felt it was very sad that this woman who had helped me should have to suffer in that way so I carried the boy to the upstairs bedroom, placed his body on the bed and prayed fervently to the Lord who restored him to life! When his mother saw him alive she lavishly praised both God and me!

Then the Lord told me that He was about to end the drought and sent me to confront king Ahab. As soon as he saw me the king accused me of being the biggest troublemaker in his kingdom. I replied that all his troubles had been caused by his own disobedience and idol worship and challenged him to bring all his people and all the so-called prophets of false god,Baal, there to Mount Camel where God would make quite clear who was the true God. He accepted the challenge and when they arrived I invited them to prepare a bull for sacrifice and to pray for their god to send a fire which would consume the offering and I would do the same to my God. The people who were there shouted their agreement!

The offerings were prepared and the king's prophets prayed and danced, working themselves up into a frenzy - but they received no answer from their god. I mocked them and their god which made them pray all the harder and they even cut themselves with knives according to their religious practice but no fire was to be seen! They continued their efforts for hours - in vain! Then it was my turn! I prayed that the Lord would let the people know that He was the one and only true God, whereupon He sent down a fire which consumed the offering I had prepared! The people were convinced and at my command, seized the false prophets and killed them!

Then I informed king Ahab that the rains were on the way and in a short time heavy rain began to fall. I wrapped my cloak tightly around myself and ran in front of the king's party all the way to Jezreel a distance in excess of twenty miles!

When the king told Jezebel what had happened she had a furious tantrum and vowed that she would have me killed. When the glow of triumph dimmed in me, I began to worry and fear for my life, and went off by myself to hide. The Lord asked why I was hiding and I told Him that I might as well be dead because Jezebel had decreed a death sentence on me. The Lord told me to stand at the top of Mount Sinai, His holy mountain, where I witnessed such a strong wind that it caused rocks to split but there was no message in it. Then there was an earthquake - but again no message. That was followed by fire - still no message! Things became very quiet and that's when I heard the still small voice of God speaking to me softly. He told me to go and anoint Hazael as the king of Syria, Jehu king of Israel and Elisha from Abel Meholah my successor as prophet. I did as He said and from then on I trained Elisha in the ways of a prophet.

King Ahab and I had yet another encounter. It was at the time when he wanted to purchase the vineyard of a man named Naboth but Naboth would not sell because it had always been in his family and he wanted to keep it that way. Jezebel had Naboth killed and king Ahab took possession of the vineyard. The Lord sent me to him and I told king Ahab in no uncertain terms of the vileness of his deed and prophesied the destruction of his entire family and the death of Jezebel, at which threat the king repented. Because of his repentance, the Lord held back the disasters on his family until after king Ahab had been killed in battle. Later Jezebel was murdered and her body eaten by dogs as the Lord had foretold.

When the time came for me to leave this earth to be with God in Heaven Elisha was most upset and although I told him to stay behind he insisted on coming with me through Bethel, Jericho and then to the river Jordan. I felt a mixture of emotions; sadness at leaving my friends and yet excitement at going to be with my loving God for all eternity. Nothing! no, nothing could be better than that.

On the way to the river Jordan we picked up a following of fifty prophets who had also been told of my immanent departure. Prompted by the Lord I took off my cloak and struck the river with it. The waters parted straight away and Elisha and I crossed over. Then we saw a chariot of fire pulled by fiery horses which came between the two of us and I was taken up to Heaven in a whirlwind. As I ascended I heard Elisha's cry from the heart and knew that God had bestowed on him the same power He had given to me and as time passed,how well he was to use it!

ELISHA

Just a few moments before, I had been trying to fight back the tears as I prepared to say goodbye to my friend and mentor, the great prophet Elijah. But I was awestruck as I witnessed the power of God. Firstly, He parted the waters of the river Jordan and then there was a chariot of fire and finally Elijah was taken up into Heaven by a whirlwind. As I saw him ascend I cried out after him with a feeling that came from deep inside. Then I was alone; Elijah's successor, remembering the amazing miracles he had performed and wondering if God would give me the same power.

In my distress I tore my cloak in two, went over to where Elijah had left his cloak, picked it up and struck the river Jordan with it as I had seen him do just a few moments earlier. Once again God parted the waters and I crossed over to where fifty other prophets had been watching. As I approached them they said, "Elisha, God has given you the same power that He gave to Elijah!" and, believing that the whirlwind would have dropped him somewhere, they set out to try to find my predecessor. Although I knew they were wasting their time they insisted and while I went to Jericho they searched for three days – but no trace of Elijah was found!

In Jericho I was asked by some men if there was anything I could do about their water which had always caused health problems. I got some salt and threw it into the source of their water supply. From that time on the water became pure and no longer caused problems to anyone's health.

On my way to Bethel, one day, a large group of boys started to make fun of my bald head - but not for long because two bears emerged from the woods and killed forty-two of them!

By that time Joram was king of Israel in succession to his father, Ahab, and Jehoshophat was king of Judah. These two kings together with the king of Edom formed an alliance to resist the attack of king Mesha of Moab. After having marched for seven days in the wilderness the armies of the alliance ran out of water and they asked me to call on the Lord for help. I was reluctant to do anything to help the others but for the sake of Jehoshophat I called for a musician in order to deepen my spiritual awareness. The message I received from the Lord was that they should dig holes in a dried up river bed and He would supply water for their needs. Next morning, after the holes had been dug, true to His word, the Lord caused the river bed to be flowing with water. He also gave victory to the three kings in their battle against the Moabites.

A little later, a widow whose husband had been a prophet came to me in desperation, explaining that a man had come to take away her two sons as slaves in payment for a debt her husband had incurred. She told me that her only possession was a little jar of olive-oil. I understood her predicament and felt compassion for her. So I told her to borrow as many empty jars as possible from her neighbours and to pour the oil from her small jar into all the others. She filled all the other larger jars from her small one. Then I told her to sell the oil, to repay her husband's debt and to keep the remaining money to live on.

There was also a well-off woman from Shunem who recognised God's power within me and because I dined at her house frequently she built a room for me on her roof. I was almost overcome by her kindness and asked my helper, Gehazi, to find out what she would like me to do for her. She informed Gehazi that there was nothing that she required but he discovered that she had wanted a son but had never had any children and as her husband was an old man she had stopped nursing that forlorn hope. I blessed her telling her that at the same time the following year she would have her much longed for child. One year later she gave birth to a son! Some years after that, I saw her coming towards me in great distress. Through her tears she told me that her son had died. As quickly as possible she, Gehazi and

I went to her house where I saw the boy lying dead on the bed. Closing the door behind me I prayed privately and sincerely to God. The boy was restored to life and his mother fell at my feet in astonishment and gratitude.

On another day, a man called Naaman who was a well respected commander of the Syrian army came to my house seeking a cure for a dreaded skin disease. At first he was reluctant to do what I said but when he eventually did wash himself seven times in the river Jordan, as I had instructed, he was cured! He recognised that it was the power of my God which had healed him and he wanted to give us a large gift but I was happy that he acknowledged that the Lord was the one and only true God and told him that no gift was necessary.

He had no sooner left on his return journey than Gehazi disgraced himself and me! He chased after Naaman and on catching up with him told him that I had changed my mind and that a gift was appropriate! Naaman was pleased to oblige. When I found out what Gehazi had done I was angry and disappointed with him and told him that as he had taken Naaman's money he would also acquire his disease. Immediately white blotches appeared on his skin.

In spite of their disloyalty to the Lord the Israelites were saved time and time again from attacks by the Syrians as God continued to display His great patience. But I, and other prophets such as Isaiah, Jeremiah and Hosea, foresaw the time when that patience would come to an end! Alas!

HEZEKIAH

After the kingdom had been split into two parts, the northern portion, called Israel,was initially ruled by Jeroboam and the southern, that is Judah, by Rehoboam. There followed a succession of kings in both regions. None in Israel had any respect for our God but there were some in Judah who honoured the Lord and some who turned away from Him. The fortunes of Judah seemed to fluctuate, growing stronger as we trusted in Him and weaker as we relied on our own ideas. It was maybe coincidence but somehow I don't think so!

I, king Hezekiah, ascended the throne of Judah at a time when both territories had suffered under the hands of wicked rulers. Idolatry was widespread and pagan altars proliferated both lands. However, the wickedness of Israel was greater than that of Judah and in the sixth year of my reign God allowed king Hoshea of Israel to be overthrown by the Assyrians. The ten northern tribes were captured and absorbed into that foreign culture and their identity became lost in history.

I was impressed by the priests of the Most High God in the temple and dedicated myself to the service of the Almighty, tearing down the pagan places of worship and insisting that my subjects observed the law of God in every way. A spiritual cleansing took place all over Judah! People called on the name of the Lord and worshipped Him once again! And the Lord was pleased! He smiled on us and we prospered!

However there was one occasion when the mighty Assyrian army attacked Judah and captured several of our cities. We tried to buy them off but it didn't work and they came in their hundreds of thousands to Jerusalem itself. Sennacherib, their Emperor, mocked our comparatively puny forces and scorned our God saying that if the gods of the other countries they had conquered had been unable to prevent his army from plundering their lands, our God could do no better.

I sought the advice of the prophet Isaiah who gave us some encouragement. He told us not to be afraid; that our God would save us from these warriors and that Sennacherib would never enter Jerusalem. That night the Lord sent an angel to the Assyrian camp and killed 185,000 of their men. The Emperor returned to Ninevah where, as he was worshipping his god, two of his own sons killed him.

Together with Isaiah, I praised Almighty God for His answer to our prayers and my joy at seeing my city safe once again was consummate - but it was short-lived. I became very ill and thought I was dying, indeed Isaiah's word from God was that I would not recover! I wept despairingly and asked the Lord to remember the way I had honoured His name and destroyed the idols throughout the land and to consider how the people worshipped Him in a manor which had not been seen since the time of king David. Isaiah, who had been leaving the palace, returned to tell me that God had heard my plea and had decided to heal me. I was to live for a further fifteen years and He promised to defend the city of Jerusalem against all enemy attacks while I was alive!

On instructions from Isaiah, my attendants made a paste from figs and put it on my sores and in a short time I made a full recovery. I am confident that God could have healed me directly without the need for a fig paste but perhaps He was telling me and everyone who hears my story that He sometimes decides to heal through medication, applied together with the power of prayer.

While I was recovering, Isaiah said that God was willing to give me a sign to show He would keep His promise. I requested that the shadow on the staircase might go back ten steps! As soon as Isaiah prayed, the shadow receded ten steps! Now, nothing is too hard for the Lord, but this was time travelling backwards! At first I thought I must be delirious but everyone else in the palace saw it too and God did fulfil His promise!

Some time later I welcomed messengers from Babylonia and, perhaps a little imprudently, displayed all the riches, spices, perfumes and military equipment in the kingdom. When they had gone Isaiah enquired about the visitors. On being informed that they had seen everything he became exasperated and told me the Lord said that when one of my descendants was in power, the men would return with their army, plunder the kingdom and take everything back to Babylonia with them. I suppose it could be said that the fate of Judah was sealed because I had tried to impress men instead of being a prudent steward of God's gifts!

JOSIAH

My father, king Amon, died when I was just eight years old and, as was the practice in those days, I succeeded him on the throne of Judah. My great-grandfather was king Hezekiah a man who obeyed the Lord, who re-instituted worship in a way which honoured our God and who curbed paganism and idolatry.

Sadly, my grandfather who was king Manasseh, was the most wicked king ever to reign over Judah. He re-introduced the worship of foreign gods, re-established pagan shrines, consulted mediums, fortune-tellers and astrologers instead of seeking God's will. He placed the obscene symbol of the heathen goddess Asherah in our holy Temple and caused the nation to commit greater sins than any king before him. He was completely lacking in justice and it has been said that the streets of Jerusalem ran with the blood of his innocent victims. One of his problems was that he had an abundance of authority but a dearth of morality! My father carried on with Manasseh's evil ways, rejecting the Lord.

As an eight year old, I didn't have a great deal of influence over the opinion of my countrymen but as I grew up I learned more about our Great God and knew that He deserved my total respect. By the time I was twenty-six, I realised that the Temple was in need of repair and so ordered it to be completely overhauled.

As the work proceeded the High Priest, Hilkiah, discovered the book of the Law which God had given to Moses and which had lain untouched for many years and it was read to me. It was amazing to hear the word of God but it was also disturbing to learn that most of God's advice and commandments had been consigned to the past. We had deprived ourselves of many of God's blessings because of our lackadaisical approach to our faith.

I was certain that if Israel, the northern kingdom, had obeyed these instructions, it would never have fallen to the Assyrians and wanted to ensure that Judah would not suffer the same fate while I was king. It was time that all the people heard from this book and so I called leaders, priests, prophets and all the people to the Temple and there in front of everyone read aloud those amazing words.

The people joined me in my dedication to God's service and I made a promise to keep all His laws and commands for the rest of my life. I then launched an all-out assault on the symbols of false gods. The Temple was cleared of all traces of artefacts relating to the worship of Astartes, Baal, the sun, moon, stars, planets etc.. Throughout the land pagan idols, altars and shrines were destroyed. The priests involved in their worship were removed and I desecrated the pagan place of worship in the valley of Hinnom where men had sacrificed their children as burnt offerings! The depravity in my country had known no limit!

All over the land and even into the northern territories, I obliterated every trace of the worship which had been so offensive to the Lord God. In Bethel I saw the tomb of the prophet who, so many years previously, had predicted to Jeroboam the destruction I would execute on this abhorrent idolatry. In recognition of his holy ministry I left his tomb untouched.

There was no record of the Passover having been celebrated for many, many years and such a momentous event as the angel of death passing over the homes of our ancestors while they were slaves in Egypt but killing the firstborn sons of the Egyptians deserved to be commemorated. In fact God had commanded it! We observed the Passover with the greatest celebration that had been seen since the time before kings were appointed to rule the land.

I made sure that every household got rid of idols and anything else which honoured false gods and I filled my mind with His laws. God was pleased with what had been done. However, the sins of Manasseh and previous kings had caused God to decide that Jerusalem would be destroyed.

Thankfully it did not happen in my lifetime but, after I died, the people under the leadership of my successors, slowly reverted to the old immoral and pagan ways. That was when king Nebuchadnezzar of Babylonia sent his army to attack Jerusalem. He was successful and desecrated the Temple, taking all the precious objects of worship. His soldiers destroyed the city walls, burnt down the Temple and took the people of Judah captive. Anyone of any importance was taken back to Babylonia but the poorest were left in Judah to farm the land. There was much weeping and wailing as our people were taken into exile and in Babylonia - Oh! how they yearned for our beautiful Temple and the fertile homeland of Judah.

What an influence the book of the Law could have had on the kings and therefore on our destiny if only they had taken the time to read it! I am certain you will agree that it was foolish of them to have the word of God so readily available and never to have read it! You wouldn't do that - would you?

DANIEL

Undoubtedly, the reason why God allowed Judah to be overrun by the Babylonians was that as a nation we had disregarded His Word and failed to respect His commandments. Nevertheless, there were little pockets of true faith where His name was honoured and I belonged to such a group. I was, however, captured and taken to Babylonia after the first wave of attack by Nebuchadnezzar and in Babylonia three of my friends and I were selected to be given training to serve in the royal court.

Our names were changed to Babylonian equivalents, my name, Daniel, becoming Belteshazzar and my friends Hananiah, Mishael and Azariah became Shadrach Meshach and Abednego respectively. Conditions, generally speaking, were good but the food provided for us was not prepared in accordance with the Law of God so we ate vegetables to prevent ourselves from becoming ritually unclean. The Lord blessed us with good health, knowledge and understanding as we studied literature and philosophy. In addition He bestowed on me the ability to explain the meaning of dreams. All four of us became part of the royal court of Nebuchadnezzar.

He was a volatile man and at times demanded what seemed impossible - like on the occasion when he had a disturbing dream and called his advisers and wise men commanding them to tell him the meaning of the dream. But he would not tell them what he had dreamt! They were ordered to tell him both the dream and its meaning! Naturally no one could oblige which caused the king to rant and rave and he ordered the execution of all his aides which included my friends and me! We prayed about the situation and that night I had a vision in which everything was revealed. I got word to the king and when I told him that my God had shown me his dream and its meaning and then explained that the dream was all about future kingdoms, he rewarded me by giving me a position of political power. I didn't forget my three friends, however, and had them placed in charge of the province of Babylonia. What pleased me most was the fact that because of this the king respected the Lord and recognised Him as the Supreme God.

I said Nebuchadnezzar was volatile and this was again proved by the fact that his 'conversion' did not last long. He had a huge gold statue built and ordered everyone to bow down and worship it otherwise they would be thrown into a fiery furnace. We, of course, could only worship our God and when it was reported to the king that Shadach, Meshach and Abednego refused to bow to his statue, the king, in a temper, asked if they thought their God would save them from death in the furnace. They replied that even if He didn't they would still not bow down to a man-made statue. His face red with anger, the king ordered the furnace to be stoked up as hot as possible, tied them up and had them thrown into the blazing fire. It was so hot that the soldiers who had the duty of carrying out the order were burned up by the blast of heat. King Nebuchadnezzar who was viewing the scene from a distance suddenly stood bolt upright! He had expected to see my three friends scream with pain and be quickly consumed by the flames! But he saw four men walking around unharmed right in the centre of the furnace! The fourth man looked like a divine being! The king immediately ordered their release. Only the three appeared, the fourth just seemed to vanish. There was no trace of heat or fire damage to Shadrah, Meshach or Abednego, only the cords which had bound them were destroyed! Once again the king praised the Lord and promoted his would-be victims to a higher position. Probably in order to appease our God.

Some time later the king had a second disturbing dream which no one could interpret. Of course, I was called in once again and when I heard his dream I was worried about telling him what it meant. How could I break the news to the king that he would lose his mind and behave like an animal for seven years? But he took it well and just one year later that is exactly what happened. Towards the end of the seven years, perhaps in one of his more lucid moments, king Nebuchadnezzar acknowledged that the Lord is the Almighty God and as he did his sanity was restored! This time he did worship the Lord!

The years passed quickly and one day a successor of Nebuchadnezzar, his son Belshazzar, held a grand banquet. He became rather jovial and showed off by ordering that the sacred cups and bowls which his father had looted from our Temple in Jerusalem be brought out and used in the celebration. What an abomination - to use these precious items to toast false gods! Suddenly and mysteriously writing appeared on the wall. As no one could understand what it meant, I was once again brought in and told king Belshazzar that this was God's warning to him that his kingdom would be split up. That very night Belshazzar was killed and a man named Darius who was a Mede seized the throne. He had the same name as the later king who ruled over the entire Persian Empire and seemed to hold me in high regard for he placed me in charge of the whole Babylonian Empire.

Apparently I had my enemies who wanted rid of me, for knowing that I worshipped the Lord they endeavoured to trick the king into having me sentenced to death! Appealing to his ego they suggested to him that, for a period of thirty days no one should be allowed to make petition to any God or official except to king Darius himself and that anyone who did so should be thrown to the lions. Believing this would add to his esteem, the king signed the order which then became irrevocable.

 It was my practice to pray three times a day before an open window which faced Jerusalem. The dedication I had for my God meant that I was not prepared to compromise my prayer times and so I continued to pray openly. These enemies of mine took great delight in reporting my behaviour to the king and demanded the specified punishment! He valued me highly and so delayed carrying out the sentence but in the end, against his will, had me thrown into the den of lions! I tensed as I saw these fierce animals! Huge and powerful and their roars were deafening! "Put your trust in the Lord" I repeated walking into their territory. I waited for the first frenzied attack! It never came! The animals accepted my presence without aggression!

In the morning it was king Darius himself who came to see what had happened to me and was delighted to find me alive and unharmed. When I explained that it was the Lord who had closed the mouths of the lions, he developed a new respect for my God and punished my accusers by condemning them to the same punishment that they had demanded for me! As soon as the lions saw them they pounced and tore them to pieces. King Darius wrote a letter to every corner of the Empire commanding everyone to show respect for my God.

During my life I had a series of visions which I recorded most of which were prophetic in nature. They dealt with future kingdoms and perhaps, some consider, even with the end of the world!

EZRA

Almost fifty years after king Nebuchadnezzar destroyed Jerusalem and took the people of Judah, who are also known as Jews, into exile, the Babylonian Empire was overthrown by Cyrus Emperor of Persia. During those fifty years the Jews drew comfort from the fact that prophets like Jeremiah and Ezekiel predicted that the time would come when we would be allowed to return to our homeland. Many years previously in the writings of the prophet Isaiah we read that a king named Cyrus would be led by God to release us from exile. In the early part of his reign, Cyrus did exactly that!

Not all the Jews decided to take advantage of this freedom however, as in some cases the comfort of established routine had a greater pull than the call of the homeland. Some 50,000 Jews, under the leadership of a man called Zerubbabel, did undertake the journey of about 800 miles, taking four months to arrive at the ruins of Jerusalem.

Cyrus had returned some of the precious objects of worship and commanded that the Temple of the Lord be rebuilt. Gold, silver, animals and other valuable items were contributed by those staying behind, in order to help the others on the journey.

As soon as they had settled in they built an altar for making sacrifices to God and the work of rebuilding the Temple started. When the foundations had been laid they celebrated, for although they knew that the new Temple might not have the glory and splendour as that built by Solomon it was, nevertheless, going to be the centre of their worship.

109

Opposition from the people who had been living in the land brought the rebuilding work to a standstill and it was not until fifteen years later when Darius was Emperor of Persia that it restarted.

Our prophets Haggai and Zechariah told our men to begin their work once again and Zerubbabel, helped by those two prophets and Joshua, the priest, led the rebuilding work. In spite of more opposition the Temple was completed four years later. The Levites among our numbers had been ordained to officiate in worship and a wonderful Passover celebration was held the year after the work was finished.

ESTHER

My name is Esther and I am Jewish. I lived in Susa, in the winter residence of king Xerxes king of the Persian empire. When Nebuchadnezzar invaded Judah and destroyed Jerusalem my people, the Jews, were taken to Babylonia as prisoners. Several years later Babylonia fell to the Persian Empire which became the largest empire ever seen up to that time. It included Sudan, Israel, Egypt and India. I was just a young woman when king Xerxes ordered that all the attractive virgins of marriageable age should be assembled and from them he would choose a wife to replace queen Vashti who had disobeyed him and had been deposed. The king chose me to be his queen.

My older cousin who had brought me up was a man named Mordecai and he discovered a plot to assassinate the king. When he told me about it I informed the king who investigated and found it to be true. King Xerxes had the plotters put to death and was grateful to Mordecai.

Later a man called Haman who was an out and out egotist became Prime Minister. One of his ancestors, king Agag, had been killed by our great prophet Samuel and as a result, he hated my people and in particular my cousin Mordecai. This was because Mordecai who honoured only God, refused to bow to him as he passed by. Haman deceived the king and got him to sign a royal decree which ordered that all the Jews in the kingdom were to be put to death. My people were in great distress and Mordecai would wear nothing but sackcloth. It was he who told me about the decree and asked me to do something about it.

We fasted for three days and prayed about the situation. Then I asked the king to come to a banquet and invite also Haman our persecutor. Haman was really pleased thinking he was being greatly honoured but as he left the palace he saw that my cousin once again refused to bow to him. He hated Mordecai so much that he planned to have him hanged on gallows he had built 22 metres high for that purpose.

The banquet was a success and so when I suggested a second one for the following night the king readily agreed. God's ways are truly awesome for that night the king could not sleep and started looking through the records. He realised that he had not rewarded Mordecai for uncovering the assassination plot and so he ordered Haman to organise a great honour for Mordecai - which truly humiliated Haman.

At the second banquet the king asked me what was the purpose of these banquets and what it was I really wanted. I told him that a man had manipulated him into signing a royal decree to have my people put to death. As realisation dawned that I would be included in the death sentence the king became furious and said "Who is this wicked man?" I told him it was Haman. The king was so angry that he had to leave the room. As soon as he did Haman threw himself on me begging for mercy. When the king returned he thought Haman was trying to rape me and had him taken out to be hanged. They used the gallows he had built for Mordecai.

Mordecai was made Prime Minister in Haman's place and the king signed another decree which gave the Jews the right to form a defensive force which they did so successfully that none of our numbers was killed. From that time my people have celebrated this deliverance in the Feast of Purim so called because it was purim (something like drawing lots) which Haman had used to determine the day on which this planned massacre was to take place.

Of all the girls in the kingdom why was I chosen to be queen?

Why was it Mordecai who discovered the plot?

Why was it that the king couldn't sleep on that particular night?

I think I see God's hand in all of this - don't you agree?

NEHEMIAH

Nehemiah, the wine steward of king Artxerxes of Persia - that was me! Part of my duty was to sample the wine before the king drank it to make sure it had not been poisoned. I suppose if I dropped down dead the king would know not to drink it - but that is being a bit dramatic! I reasoned that no one who wanted to kill the king would poison his wine knowing that I would be testing it first so the job was not as hazardous as it might seem.

I was one of the Jews living in the Persian Empire but my heart was in the land of my fathers where the Temple had been rebuilt and where Ezra, a studious scholar and priest had gone some thirteen years previously. One day my brother, Hanani, who had been living in Jerusalem, returned and reported that although the Temple was being honoured and Ezra was teaching everyone the Law of God, the city walls and the city itself were in a state of desolation and our people living there were vulnerable to any foreign raiders.

It made me very sad to think of the city that had once been the jewel in the crown of Judah lying in so much rubble. My depression could not be hidden and I was alarmed when the king noticed how unhappy I appeared to be. He questioned me and I explained my feeling of despair whereupon he gave me permission to travel to Jerusalem in order to organise the reconstruction of the city and authorised a royal escort to accompany me. He also gave me letters which instructed that I should be given free passage to Judah and that I should be supplied with all the wood I required in the restoration of the city.

Sanballat, from Beth Horon, and Tobiah, from Ammon, were enemies of the Jews and were not pleased to learn that I had been appointed Governor of Judah on the authority of the king. God,

114

however, had inspired me to rebuild the city and a few days after my arrival, I went out in the middle of the night to survey the broken walls and gates of the city. A plan for reconstructing them was forming in my mind.

I spoke to my fellows Jews with such enthusiasm that they, to a man, wanted to proceed. They were catching the vision! "Let's get started!" they shouted! Each family or group of families was put in charge of rebuilding a section of the walls. As we might have expected, Sanballat and Tobiah scorned our efforts, telling us that we were undertaking an impossible task! I replied that God was in our work and that we would succeed! Our workers were not discouraged by their taunts.

Day after day we worked with great dedication and each day saw the walls grow a little higher, stronger and the gaps begin to close! Everyone played their part, ordinary men, priests, officials, old and young and the walls soon reached half their full height. Again our two enemies ridiculed our efforts but I detected a note of concern in their mockery.

When they saw how well we were progressing they plotted with the people of Arabia, Ammon and Ashdod to attack Jerusalem! I organised weapons for our workers and positioned them in places where we were still vulnerable. It did slow us down a little, for half our number had to be on guard in case of attack while the other half continued to build the walls. I ordered that even those who were working had to carry weapons. The people were obviously worried but I reminded them of our God's power and told them He was on our side. The way we were set up discouraged our enemies from putting their plan into action and we worked with a God inspired fervour which enabled us to complete the walls within two months. When the completed project was surveyed it was hard to believe just how much we had achieved in such a short time. Our enemies also realised that God must have had a hand in it.

During our labour it was brought to my attention that the poorer Jews were becoming destitute and so I chastised the better off for their lack of consideration. The more prosperous among our people changed their ways, offering relief to the poor. Personally, I did not take advantage of the finances on offer to me as Governor of the region, choosing to set the example of frugal living instead of enjoying affluence.

One of the highlights of that period was when all the people of Israel assembled in front of the Temple and asked Ezra to read the word of God to them. He did so for hours on end and the people had an insatiable appetite for His instruction. They unanimously agreed to obey God's commands, to observe the Sabbath as a day dedicated to Him, to marry no foreign women and to provide funds for the Levites, the priests, for the upkeep of the Temple and everything involved in our worship. I remained in Jerusalem for twelve years before returning to Babylonia in order to give a report to king Artaxerxes.

When I returned to Jerusalem, after having given my report to the king, Tobiah had been given permission, by Eliashib the priest, to use a room in the Temple and the Temple itself was being neglected. I was livid, threw out all Tobiah's belongings, ordered that the room should be ritually cleansed and laid down rules making sure that no aspect of our worship would ever again be disregarded.

The prophet Habakkuk was perplexed that God should have chosen heathen nations to discipline His chosen people for it took the purging by the Babylonians and the collaboration of the Persians for us to eventually surrender to God's will but I think I can safely say that we Jews, as a nation, never again worshipped idols or false gods.

<u>GOD'S WORD REVISITED – PART TWO</u>

<u>THE NEW TESTAMENT</u>

	PAGE NUMBER
1. VIRGIN MARY	119.
2. JOHN THE BAPTIST	122.
3. PETER	125.
4. JAMES	129.
5. JOHN	132.
6. MARTHA	136.
7. THE BOY WITH 5 LOAVES AND 2 FISH.	139.
8. THE MAN BORN BLIND	142.
9. THE LEPER	145.
10. JAIRUS	148.
11. ZACCHEUS	151.
12. PONTIUS PILATE	153.

13. BARABBAS   156.

14. MARY MAGDALENE   159.

15. JOSEPH OF ARIMATHEA   162.

16. DOUBTING THOMAS   165.

17. STEPHEN   168.

18. PHILIP   171.

19. CORNELIUS   174.

20. PAUL   177.

21. TIMOTHY   180.

22. BARNABAS   183.

VIRGIN MARY

I know my story is hard to believe and when I tell you that my name is Mary and that I was a virgin when I had my first child you will understand why. I was living in Nazareth which, at that time, was under Roman occupation. One day when I was just a girl and on my own something happened that you will find hard to accept but please believe me - it really is true. A Heavenly being, an angel named Gabriel, appeared to me and told me I would have a baby although I had never known a man. It was unbelievable but something about him told me he was sincere. I was engaged at the time to a man called Joseph. How could I tell him - and what would my family say - and my friends? No doubt I would be regarded as the village slut. Yes me! - always so determined to stand on the high moral ground. Oh! How the gossips would love this! Yet it was God's will; and my devotion to Him mattered more than my reputation. After all He knows best.

Joseph was devastated when I told him that the power of the Holy Spirit had caused a baby to be conceived in me. I don't think that he was willing to accept that and good man that he was he wanted to break off our engagement quietly so that I would not be humiliated but the Lord spoke to him in a dream telling him it was true that the child to be born was indeed God's own son. I was so happy when we married after all. Part of me was worried about the opinions of the townsfolk but another, greater part, sang praise to God for choosing me for this most unique event in all of human history - giving birth to the son of God!

We had to go to Bethlehem, the town of Joseph's ancestor David, to register in a census ordered by Emperor Augustus and as we arrived I went into labour. The inns were full up and so I gave birth in a stable.

He was a lovely child but even I was surprised when shepherds and wise men came to give him gifts and adoration. Apparently there was a bright star in the sky which was God's indication to them that the Messiah had been born. How I treasured these memories!!

As he grew up he seemed somehow to know that he was God's son and no mother ever had a better child. His intelligence and knowledge soon far outstripped mine but he always wanted to help and what a considerate child he was - and so compassionate! There was one time however, when he worried me greatly. It was when we had gone as a large group on our annual trip to celebrate the Passover in Jerusalem and on the way back home Joseph and I realised that Jesus was missing from our party. We returned to the city and searched for two days in vain! On the third day we found him in the Temple talking to the teachers who were amazed at his intelligence and knowledge. He was only twelve years old at the time and we scolded him saying that we had looked all over Jerusalem for him. He appeared to be surprised and replied that we should have known he would be in his Father's house. The implication of this comment staggered me but I was just so relieved to find him again!

When he grew to manhood his knowledge and love of the scriptures had to have an outlet and he began his own ministry. I wasn't at all surprised at his first public miracle - changing water into wine but I must admit that some of the other things he did amazed even me - things like restoring sight to a man born blind, healing the lame and bringing people back from the dead.

I was so happy he was my son and proud, and I could believe the things that were prophesied about him but I worried that the High Priests and the Pharisees opposed and condemned him. Something else worried me - it was what a God inspired man named Simeon prophesied when Jesus was just a baby. He said my son Jesus was chosen by God but that sorrow like a sword would pierce my soul. I had no idea how true that was to be until the day the crowd screamed "CRUCIFY HIM!!!" The nails that pierced his hands and feet pierced my heart also!! But even on the cross he had dignity in his agony. How I wished I could have taken his place at least for a while to ease his suffering. Now, of course I realise that, that was not possible because only the perfect one could be God's own sacrifice to pay the price for the sins of the whole of mankind. It still hurts me to think he went through all that and yet for so many people he did it for nothing. So I would like to say that if you haven't yet accepted his sacrifice on your behalf now is the time to do it!

Even on the cross his thoughts were for others - he told his beloved disciple John to look after me as he would his own mother - and that was shortly before he died such was his love for me. And do you know something? He loves you every bit as much!!!

JOHN THE BAPTIST

My parents were very old when I was born and my mother often sat me on her knee and told me about the events leading up to my birth. It seems that she had all but given up hope of having any children when one day my father, Zechariah, while proceeding with his priestly duties in the temple, was visited by the angel of God who told him that he would be the father of a son whom God would use mightily to prepare the way for the Lord. The message of the prophet Elijah would be proclaimed once again over all the land through this son whose name was to be John.

My father doubted the angel's message and was reprimanded - he would be unable to speak until I was born! Things happened just as the angel had said and I was conceived.

When my mother was six months pregnant she was visited by Mary, a close relative, who herself was pregnant by the miraculous power of the Holy Spirit - Mary was to give birth to the Saviour! My mother, Elizabeth, told me that as soon as Mary appeared, I seemed to sense, even while in the womb, the presence of the embryonic Lord, for I moved powerfully and my mother was full of delight and praise!

A week after my birth the Jewish priests came to perform the rite of circumcision and to officially name me. They were about to give me my father's name when my mother, remembering the angel's words, told them my name was to be John! They argued that no one in the family had that name whereupon my father wrote on a slate " His name is John!" Immediately, my father regained the power of speech - and so I was named.

When I grew up I felt a most definite urge from the Lord to proclaim to the world at large the message of repentance for sins and to call people everywhere to be baptised as a sign that they wished to turn away from evil and receive forgiveness. My lifestyle, diet and clothes were a little unconventional but I required very little to live on and prayed constantly to God. He inspired me to such an extent that huge crowds came to be baptised and I had several disciples helping me. Many of those who heard me proclaim God's message believed that I was the Messiah but I knew that someone greater than me was about to come on the scene!

One day, while baptising in the river Jordan, I saw the Lord! His name was Jesus, the offspring of Mary and the Son of God.! He came forward to be baptised. I recognised His greatness and felt completely inadequate for He had the greater authority. I tried to say that as He was without sin He did not require this ritual. Very gently He told me to let it be this way for the present! What a privilege it was to baptise Him! As soon as He emerged from the water I saw the Holy Spirit descend on Him and heard God's voice from Heaven saying that Jesus was the beloved son with whom He was well pleased! What an experience! From then on I directed all who were baptised by me to go to Him.

I was not the kind of man who kept quiet when I saw wrong-doing and sometimes condemned religious leaders for their self righteousness and I was arrested for telling Herod, our ruler by Roman appointment, that he had broken our law by taking Herodias, his brother Philip's wife, to be his own wife. Herod often had me brought from my prison cell to talk about questions of faith. He seemed to enjoy these conversations but I don't think he quite knew what to do with me. Herodias, however, hated me for she loved the honour of her position and felt threaten. She was a cunning, dangerous woman!

One day, Herod was celebrating his birthday and held a great party. Salome, who was Herodias' daughter by Philip, danced before the group and was so entrancing that Herod rashly told her that he would reward her by giving her whatever she asked. She consulted with her mother who told her to request my head on a platter! Herod was trapped - he didn't want to have me killed but he had made a promise in front of all his guests! I was beheaded!

My life on earth had come to an end but Jesus spoke of me in the most glowing of terms likening me to the great prophet Elijah. I am certain that the spirit of Elijah was with me as I proclaimed the same message that he would have proclaimed had he been on earth at that time:-

"Repent for the Kingdom of Heaven is at hand!"

PETER

"And you will be known as Cephas" Jesus said to me. The Greek equivalent of the Aramaic word 'Cephas' can be translated as the name Peter and means "rock". A rock! Me? Perhaps Jesus could see the potential in me but I felt more impulsive and impetuous than rock-like!

It all started when my brother Andrew and I had been fishing in Lake Galilee. Jesus came by and called us to follow Him so that He could teach us to become fishers of men. He had a certain bearing and a calm authority which permitted no argument. I could see right away that He was a man of God and fell on my knees telling Him to go away for I was stained with sin! He seemed to look into the very recess of my heart and I got the impression that He already knew the kind of man I was.

When He also called our co-workers James and John who were the sons of Zebedee, all four of us left our nets and became His disciples such was the force of His magnetic appeal. Later, the inner group of His disciples grew to twelve in number and for almost three years we saw Him in action, learned from Him and came to love Him as He showed His concern and compassion for the great and the small alike. We saw Him perform miracle after miracle helping people, healing them and even bringing the dead back to life. At first we were astounded but as time passed we learned to accept His miraculous power as something which had been given Him by God whom He called His Father.

His fame began to spread and when He preached, people came from miles around to listen to His words and to see Him heal the infirm. He taught the crowds about the Kingdom of God and turned established religious thinking on its head. He emphasised how important it was that words and actions should be the product of a pure heart and not be displayed for the sake of mere appearance.

The Jewish leaders were upset when He indicated that they were more interested in being clean on the outside than on the inside. He told them bluntly that they were behaving like hypocrites, puffed up with personal grandeur as they looked down on ordinary people.

Whenever He preached He did so by telling stories, called parables, about everyday life which illustrated His points clearly. The people loved Him and some thought that He might be the leader who would free us from the rule of our Roman persecutors. But Jesus said that His Kingdom did not belong to this world and that we should give to Caesar what belonged to Caesar and, more importantly, give to God what belonged to God!

I remember the time when we all thought that He was a ghost. It was early in the morning and the rest of us were in a boat in the middle of Lake Galillee rowing hard against the wind. All of a sudden we saw this figure which appeared to be walking on the water. We were terrified until we realised it was Jesus. We could hardly believe our eyes! I asked Him if I could also walk on the water and He told me to come out of the boat and when I did, I seemed to float standing up! It was truly astounding but as I became aware of the wind and waves I took my eyes off Jesus and started to sink. He helped me into the boat and to safety.

Slowly we all began to realise that He was the son of God! Sometimes I wished He would not be so frank in His condemnation of self-righteous religious leaders but He would never compromise His Father's word! The High Priest and the Pharisees had the responsibility of administering our Jewish faith but when they realised how popular Jesus had become they were jealous and His claim that God was His Father offended them. On one occasion He caused us a great deal of concern as He revealed that He must go to Jerusalem where He would be persecuted and put to death but after three days He would rise from the tomb. We tried to dissuade Him from going there but He told us that it was His Father's will - that was the end of the discussion!

It was a Sunday when He rode into Jerusalem on the back of the colt of an ass just as the ancient scriptures foretold. Men and women lined the road, shouted His praise, placed palm leaves in His track to honour Him and joyfully sang encouragement. Christians were later to celebrate His triumphant entry into Jerusalem in what is called Palm Sunday. When He came to the Temple He was full of indignation as He saw merchants selling animals for the sacrifice at exorbitant prices and exchanging currency at inflated rates. They were bent on making a huge profit out of the common man's faith! Jesus chased them from the forecourt of the Temple, overturned the tables of the money-changers and released several of the animals. I admired His courage and dedication to His Father's house.

It was not long before the Jewish authorities had Him arrested and brought to trial on the charge of blasphemy. I had told Jesus that I loved Him and was prepared to die with Him - after all I was the "rock"! Some rock! I was challenged by some of the locals on the night of His arrest and three times denied that I even knew Him - and then the cock crowed! I remembered that Jesus had predicted my denials would happen before the cock crowed and went off by myself to cry my heart out!

All of us were devastated on the Friday when, after a mockery of a trial, He was put to death on a cross. We were devoid of all energy and motivation at that point but on Sunday we discovered that He had been resurrected never to die again! He told us to stay in Jerusalem until the power of the Spirit came upon us.

It was about fifty days after His death, and after He had ascended to His Father in Heaven, that it happened! We were sitting around consoling each other when suddenly the building we were in started to shake and we saw tongues of fire alight on each one of us. We were so full of the joy of the Lord that although it was early in the day, we went straight out and started to preach the word of God with such power that thousands of people dedicated their lives to His service and amazingly, the foreigners who were there all heard us speak in their own language! We then understood that this was the power for which Jesus had told us to wait in Jerusalem.

From that day we were changed men, indeed the world was was a changed place as God let loose His Spirit and in spite of opposition and persecution the Christian message was carried all over the world. It was then that I began to exhibit the rock-like character which Jesus had implied was inherent in me - but it took the power of the Spirit to bring it out! Many converts to Christianity experienced God's power, changing weakness into strength and they received spiritual gifts which they were happy to use in willing service to Him.

I was instrumental in spreading that message and am happy to say that in conjunction with the other apostles, including a former Pharisee called Paul, the salvation that Jesus offers freely to all who accept His teaching was made known to all the world. It was my delight to feel the Spirit's power as I proclaimed that message. In the end I too was put to death on a cross but I did not feel worthy to share the same death as my Master and so I requested that I be crucified upside down. The request was granted and I thought nothing of dying, in the knowledge of the glory which was awaiting me.

Everyone has to make decisions from time to time which can affect their whole lives and I am happy that I looked at Jesus as I made the decision to say 'yes' to becoming a fisher of men but then keeping my eyes on Him helped me make the right decision on many, many occasions!

JAMES

I was there when Jesus began His ministry by calling Andrew, Peter, my brother John and myself, James, to follow Him and become His disciples. He increased that number to twelve by recruiting Philip, Bartholomew, Thomas, Matthew, Thadaeus, another James, Simon (not Simon Peter) and lastly Judas who became the keeper of our funds and who was later to betray Him.

John and I had a lot to learn for we had both inherited a family trait - we were hot tempered and had short fuses, so much so that Jesus nick-named us the Sons of Thunder. I remember on one occasion as we came into Samaria we were not welcomed there and John and I, in annoyance, wanted to call down fire from Heaven to destroy the place. Jesus rebuked us gently making us consider what kind of spirit was controlling our thoughts. It did make a difference to our attitude.

I was there to witness our Master being glorified. Jesus, Peter, John and I had gone up a hill to pray and as we did we suddenly became aware of a change taking place in Jesus! His clothes became whiter than white and even His face changed its appearance. Then we saw two other men standing there shining with the glory of God. We learned that they were Moses and Elijah who had been sent to strengthen Jesus for the ordeal He was soon to face. Moments later a cloud shielded us from the sun. It was eerie to say the least! A voice spoke from the cloud telling us that Jesus was God's son and that we should do as He said! After that, we had no doubt that Jesus was the Christ!

I was there when a woman who had severe bleeding touched Jesus' cloak and was immediately healed and also just a short time later when He brought a twelve year old girl back to life! I was there when

He fed 5000 men with just five loaves and two fish and explained to us, the disciples, that He was the bread of life.

I was there when He preached what has become known as the Sermon on the Mount or the Beatitudes where he said that God would bless the poor, the hungry, those who are sad, the humble, those who are hated, rejected and insulted for following Him, those who show mercy, the poor in heart, the peacemakers and those who are persecuted. He told such people to hold on to their faith as they would receive a great reward in Heaven. It was made clear that Heaven itself was such a glorious reward that it was beyond our ability to earn and yet Jesus offered it freely to everyone who accepted Him in faith, but a faith that is shown to be true by the way we put it into action.

I was there to hear Him say that the greatest commandment was to love the Lord our God with all our heart, soul and mind and the second greatest was to love our neighbours as ourselves.

I was there when my mother pressed John and I to request positions of power in His coming kingdom. We were not really surprised to hear Him say that these matters would be decided by His Father. He showed us that if we wanted to be the greatest we should make ourselves the least and He demonstrated this principle when He began to wash the feet of all His disciples. This was the task of a lowly slave but the Master chose to do it Himself. At that point Peter, ever the outspoken one, said that he would not allow Jesus to perform that menial task on him but Jesus said that if he didn't, then Peter could no longer be His disciple. All credit to Peter, he did not then behave in a petty way but immediately humbled himself and told Jesus that if that was the case He could wash his hands and head also.

I was there when Jesus walked on water, when He restored sight to the blind, healed lepers and cured men who were paralysed. Oh; but there were so many things He did which only the Son of God could do!

Sadly, I was there when Jesus was put to death and I witnessed firstly, a darkness spread across the land and then an earthquake as He died. It seemed like God's grief was being expressed in nature for all to see!

But I was also there when the resurrected Christ appeared to His disciples and when we were filled with the Spirit's power, all of us becoming evangelistic in nature. Then whenever we spoke about Jesus, many people accepted the truth about Him and turned away from sinful living. It was a wonderful feeling being able to tell everyone that, no matter what they had done, if they had truly repented and accepted that Jesus had paid the penalty for their sins they were washed clean and in living according to the words of Jesus, they could spend eternity in the Heavenly world!

I was there to see the Church of Christ spread throughout the world by the power of His Spirit as Peter, John and I led the group of apostles in their efforts. However, king Herod instituted a series of persecutions against our movement during which I was taken captive and put to death by the sword. This action pleased the Jews but warned the other followers of the Faith that they must take steps to prevent the same thing happening to them. I am happy to think that although all the apostles were willing to give their lives for Jesus, my death may have made them more vigilant, gaining the time necessary to establish the foundation of His Church on earth!

JOHN

I became known as John the apostle Jesus loved. Now, Jesus was a man whose purity and compassion inspired love but I am not certain what it was about me that caused Him to like me so much. Perhaps it was because I was the youngest of the diciples. I was every bit as hot-headed as my brother James but perhaps Jesus saw the person I could become. It probably amused Him to see the way I reacted to things which irritated me but maybe He spotted that there was honesty in my angry outbursts.

However, the more I associated with Jesus, heard His words and saw his power, the more He cooled the heat of my anger and fanned the flames of love in my soul. I began to realise how much more pleasant it is, to give expression to love rather than to temper, and I eventually became a man obsessed by giving and receiving unconditional love. Jesus loved me and the other disciples in that unconditional way, indeed, He loved the whole world but the love for His Father surpassed every other thing.

Sometimes He spoke bluntly as and when the occasion demanded and never watered down His Father's word. For example; a rich young ruler once asked Jesus what he must do to belong to the Kingdom of Heaven. When Jesus told him he must obey the commandments, the rich young man declared that from his childhood he had always observed them. Jesus saw that he was being truthful but also that fondness for his material goods held back his spiritual progress and so He told the young man that he should sell what he had, give the money to the poor and join our group . The young man went away feeling very unhappy because he could not give up his riches. How easy it would have been to reassure the young man that he was doing well but Jesus' concern went far beyond earthly reward.

No, He did not succumb to telling His listeners what they wanted to hear but always pointed them in the right direction and He was never in any doubt, never in two minds. It was as if the word of God was engraved into the very fabric of His being and sometimes He would say things that really made you think. Nicodemus found that out! When Jesus told him " You must be born again to see the Kingdom of God", Nicodemus was certainly puzzled but eventually understood the statement to mean that just as a person is born physically and lives in a physical world so he must also come to life in a spiritual way and live according to the promptings of God's Spirit.

I learned that Jesus was indeed the Son of God, the incarnate Word of God, the light of the world and the Saviour of mankind and all the things He said were precious to me. Things like; that to whoever believed in Him, death was not the end but the beginning of Eternal Life in Heaven; and that He was the way, the truth and the life and no one could come to the Father except through Him. But He always made it quite clear that He testified only to what His Father had told Him.

There was one time when His message was so strong that many in the crowds turned away from Him and He asked if we, His disciples, wanted to give up on Him too. Peter was the one who voiced the thoughts in all of our minds when he said that there was no one else who had the words that led to Eternal Life. And then there was the time when Jesus surprised us by saying that one of us would betray Him. That declaration was repeated on the night before His death while we were celebrating Passover in an upper room. I was sitting beside Jesus when He made the statement and we all wondered which of us He had in mind. Peter whispered to me to ask Jesus who the traitor would be and when I did, Judas Iscariot was indicated! Jesus instructed us that in future whenever we ate the bread and drank the wine we should remember His body and His blood. What He meant became clear the next day and the sacrament of Communion, or the Eucharist, became established in Christian Churches, in His memory.

Judas had been given thirty pieces of silver to point Jesus out to the Roman soldiers and the Temple guards, who had been sent to arrest Him on the charge of blasphemy because He claimed to be the Son of God. Jesus was arrested and Peter, impulsive as ever, pulled out his sword and sliced off the ear of the High Priest's slave but Jesus calmed Peter, encouraged him to put his sword away and healed the man's ear telling Peter that the immanent suffering was in accordance with His Father's will.

His trial was a stop - start affair going from one place to another but eventually Pontius Pilate the Roman governor yielded to the desire of the crowd, which had been skilfully manipulated by the High Priest, and sentenced Jesus to be crucified! What a tortuous death! The pain He endured was beyond imagination and yet I knew that He could have used His Godly power to come down from the cross if He had so chosen. But I also knew that in His agony He was taking upon Himself the sins of the world and in a sense it was my sins and yours which were being crucified! Knowing that the pain He felt, was the price for my forgiveness brought tears to my eyes and I stood in wonder at His going through wave after wave of searing torture for me.

The pain could have been the only thought in His mind - but then it dawned on me! There must have been one thing greater, in the mind of my beloved Saviour, than the pain - His Love!!! His Love for me, for you and for His Father was what enabled Him to endure the agony of the cross! Being aware of that, I could never regard His sacrifice as a cheap thing. It became the most important event in my life! The Son of God died for me! Yes; the Son of God died for you too!

The heartbreak I experienced at seeing Him suffer was as nothing compared to what He underwent and yet in the midst of all that suffering He showed concern for Mary, His mother, by telling me to look after her for Him. When He was gone I treated Mary as I would my own mother. I took her eventually to Ephesus where we lived in a little house at the top of a hill overlooking the town.

There were times after that when I had to endure hardships and suffering of my own but when I thought of the cross on which Jesus Christ died I was always reassured of God's sustaining love!

MARTHA

I was one of those people who like to feel everything was organised and under control and that all the loose ends were tied up. Usually I felt it was my responsibility to make things run smoothly, but with that came the feeling of pressure and if things were not going according to plan, I got quite stressed.

It was like that one day when Jesus was in my house. Jesus, I should say was someone my sister, Mary and my brother, Lazarus and I considered to be an especially good friend and when He was in the area, we often invited Him to dine with us.

We lived in Bethany, a small village not two miles from Jerusalem. On the day in question I was slaving away in the kitchen preparing the food and getting up tight because no one was willing to assist me. Mary was sitting at Jesus' feet listening rapturously to every word He said. I would have liked to do that too but someone had to do the housework and the cooking. I found myself becoming annoyed with Mary for not helping and dropped a few hints that she ought to lend a hand but they were ignored.

Finally my stress built up to such a level that I snapped and showed my irritation with Mary for her lack of consideration and with Jesus for encouraging her. "Lord", I said, "don't you care that I have been left to do all the work by myself. Won't you ask Mary to help me?". Jesus looked at me with that kind, loving and yet reproving expression and said, "Oh, Martha, Martha why do you fret so much? Don't be so concerned about these mundane tasks. The Kingdom of Heaven is so much more important. Mary, in choosing to listen to my words has made the right choice. I won't discourage her interest in Heavenly matters." I felt like saying, "that is all very well but if we all did that then nothing on earth would get done", but inside I knew what He meant:- to get my priorities in order. We cooked and cleaned every day but could only hear about the Kingdom of Heaven when He was here. From then on I did list my priorities and paradoxically seemed to have more time to handle these ordinary, every day tasks and did so with less stress.

Some time later, Lazarus, our brother became seriously ill. Mary and I sent a message to Jesus telling Him about Lazarus and asking Him to come quickly. He did not arrive for several days during which time our brother died! My sister and I grieved sorely as Lazarus' body was placed in a tomb - a cave with a large rock rolled over the entrance.

When Jesus finally appeared I went to meet Him while Mary stayed home mourning. It was obvious from all the weeping and wailing of our neighbours that Lazarus was dead. "Lord, if only you had come sooner you could have healed him." I said. Jesus replied that Lazarus would rise to life. I thought He meant at Judgement Day but He said that He was the resurrection and the Life giving me the impression that He had control over life and death. I hurried back to tell Mary that Jesus was asking for her. She went to Jesus and through her tears said what I had implied earlier that if only He had come sooner Lazarus would not have died!

Jesus looked around and saw the sadness of all those who were present. He was so touched by their emotions and by His personal feelings for my brother that I saw tears fall from His face. We went to where Lazarus was buried and Jesus said to remove the rock covering the entrance to the tomb. "But Lord", I warned, "there will be a terrible smell of rotting flesh - he has been in there for four days!" However, the rock was removed and Jesus told us we were about to see God's glory. He prayed to His Father and then shouted, "Lazarus! Come out!" Seconds later my brother emerged, restored to life, with some of the grave clothes still wrapped round him. He lived for many years after that.

One final incident I would like to relate was when, just one week before His death, Mary anointed Jesus' feet with one of her most precious possessions - a jar of very expensive perfume! She then dried His feet with her hair. Judas Iscariot condemned the action as a great waste and suggested that the perfume could have been sold and the money given to the poor. I was suspicious of his motives but Jesus silenced him by indicating that, in a sense, Mary was preparing His body for burial. A week later we discovered how true that was!

After His death I remembered all He had taught us about having faith in Him and about His death being the perfect sacrifice for the sins of the world. I gratefully accepted the redemption He offered freely to me and though I may have lost a dear friend, I found a loving Saviour!

THE BOY WITH FIVE LOAVES AND TWO FISH

I became one of the most famous boys in the whole of the Bible and all because I had a basket with five barley loaves and two fish. It happened like this:-

I was on my way home with a basket containing the loaves and fish when I noticed a large crowd of people standing on a hillside watching and listening attentively to a man called Jesus who was healing everyone who had any kind of malady.

When He started to preach it was spellbinding! He spoke in terms that even a boy like me could understand although I suspected there was a deeper meaning which was beyond me at that time. Everyone was silent as we heard Him speak with an authority that defied contradiction. Every word He spoke seemed to have a life of its own. His ideas were fresh and I listened with a feeling inside me which I can only describe as joy. He was positively magnetic and the time just flew by.

In fact, it was well into the evening before I realised it and then I heard His helpers discuss food. They had made no provision to feed the crowd and it would take more money than they had to buy enough food to satisfy such a large number. There must have been 5000 men and when you add on the women and children it must have just about doubled that number. However, He had really won me over and I felt I wanted to help in some small way so I approached one of His men, a man I later discovered was named Andrew, and told him that I could let them have the five loaves and two fish in my basket. I know that sounds silly - how could that small amount of food even begin to be shared among a multitude like the one

139

gathered on that hill? But in my heart I wanted to do something to help Him. Andrew went to Jesus and told Him about my food but added the sceptical thought which I shared - that it wasn't anywhere near enough! Nevertheless, Jesus smiled at me, took the food and indicated that it would be sufficient. I ought to have thought that to feed the crowd with those meagre supplies would be impossible but I somehow felt that nothing was beyond Him.

Jesus asked the crowd to sit down on the grassy slopes in manageable groups and then proceeded to do something I have never forgotten. He started to break the loaves and give a portion to His helpers to pass on to each of the groups. He did the same with the fish but the amazing thing was that He didn't run out of either! The more He gave away the more the food just seemed to regenerate. It took a long time to feed the crowd and when we had all had our fill the leftovers were gathered up in baskets. Twelve baskets were filled with what was left.

At first, most people hadn't realised that anything out of the ordinary was happening but when they did they started to talk among themselves. I heard some of the more knowledgeable ones liken this experience to an incident in the life of the great prophet, Elijah. They said that Elijah had gone to a poor widow at the time of a great famine. The widow had only a little oil and flour but Elijah assured her that her meagre supplies would not run out until the famine was over - and they didn't. Others in the crowd mentioned Elijah's successor, Elisha who, they said, helped another poor widow by telling her to take her only remaining asset which was a small jar of oil and pour it into empty jars which she had borrowed from her neighbours. She filled all the large jars from her small jar. So it was that the people in the crowd likened Jesus to the great prophets of long ago. As time passed I, and hopefully they, learned that Jesus was far greater than any prophet who had ever lived and ever would live.

The time came for me to return home that night and on my way I began to wonder what my mother would say when she learned I had given away my food but when I described what had happened, I saw a smile pass across her lips and realised that she thought my story was merely the vivid imagination of her son. I knew that it was no use trying to convince her but somehow I felt that in time she would come to believe.

When I became a man I often heard people say that they felt inadequate and that they had so little to contribute that what they could offer scarcely seemed worthwhile. Then I would tell them about a little boy who gave the Lord a small amount of food which He was able to use in a mighty way! Thank You Jesus!

THE MAN BORN BLIND

When my family and friends spoke about the blue of the sea, the green of the grass, birds flying in the sky and about the sun, moon and stars in the heavens, I could only guess at what they meant. That was the great disadvantage of being born blind. My fingertips became my eyes, for anything which I touched could be visualised. Unfortunately as I grew to manhood, I was unable to find any employment which would provide me with a livelihood and therefore was forced to resort to begging in Jerusalem.

One day I had an encounter with a man called Jesus, which changed my life completely. His disciples had noticed me and asked Him why I had been born blind and Jesus replied that it was so that God's glory could be revealed! He then spat on the ground and made some mud which He spread on my eyes. "Go and wash in the Pool of Siloam." He said. I found the Pool, knelt down and washed the mud off my eyes. As soon as I did, I experienced something I had never known before. I began to be aware of light and dark, and as I opened my eyes, I saw colours! Then there were shapes; people; the land; trees; flowers; the sky! So that was what blue looked like, I marvelled. Birds were flying beneath a silvery white cloud! I was completely overwhelmed by the beauty and variety of all I saw and even with the faces of the people passing by! I had touched the faces of my family and had an idea of what features looked like but had no concept of facial expressions. One person was happy, another sad and the eyes of yet another were gleaming with excitement - touching had not begun to convey that!

My eyes darted here and there trying to take in everything at once. I had not anticipated just how wonderful creation was and hoped I would never become so accustomed to its beauty that it would be taken for granted! Only a God of infinite power and imagination could have created all this splendour.

It was while in that state of dazed wonder that my neighbours spotted me and could not believe what they saw! I had to confirm that it really was me - the man who had been blind from birth! They paraded me in front of the Pharisees who questioned me about how I had been given my sight. I told them that the man, Jesus, had made some mud, rubbed it on my eyes and told me to wash it off and that as soon as this had been done, I was able to see! Rather surprisingly they appeared to be unhappy about my story.

It was suggested by some of the Pharisees that Jesus could not be a man of God because He had carried out this miracle on the Sabbath which was contrary to the law of God. I was not convinced, as I knew that the Sabbath should be used for the Lord's glory and Jesus had certainly revealed that glory to me. The Pharisees had added so many rules of their own making that it had become a day of severe restrictions and it was evident that they were in danger of worshipping the Sabbath rather than the Lord of the Sabbath.

Some of the others admitted that a sinful man was unlikely to be able to perform a miracle like this. They asked for my opinion of Jesus and, without hesitation, I declared that He was a man of God! Suspicion spread across their faces and they questioned my parents, doubting that I had been born blind. Having confirmed my congenital disability, my parents advised them to ask me the questions, as I was old enough to speak for myself. Again they questioned me and instructed me to tell the truth, claiming that Jesus was a sinner. I responded by saying "I only know that I was blind but now I can see!". Irritation and frustration crept into my voice when they asked me once more to explain what had happened that enabled me to see. I replied that they had already been told and it was beginning to sound as if they would like to become His disciples themselves. This made them very angry and we started to argue, which resulted in my being expelled from the synagogue.

143

When Jesus learned of this, He searched me out and I confessed my faith in Him. I may have been shown the door of the synagogue by the Pharisees but the gates of Heaven had been opened to me by Jesus! He went on to tell a parable about a good shepherd who loved his sheep, and He made it clear that He was the Good Shepherd sent by God and was willing to die for His sheep who were, in fact, those who accepted Him as their Lord and Saviour.

Instinctively, I knew He was speaking the truth and realised that the only way into God's presence was through Jesus, His Son. Just a short time previously, He had enabled me to see physically, and there He was opening my spiritual eyes! My mind boggled; the beauty of visible creation was enhanced by the joy of the intangible salvation I had found in Him.

In a way, I felt sorry for the Pharisees as, in a sense, they lived in self-imposed darkness and in their stubborn pride, refused to accept the light which Jesus was only too willing to impart. I pray that people like that might relax their grip on the burden of self glorification in order that they might experience the greater glory of Christ.

THE LEPER

You have to be one to know how bad it can be - a leper that is. That slow degeneration of body which becomes a long drawn out death sentence! Of course, I wasn't always a leper but the experience of this illness made those past few years seem like an eternity! I remember how it started - just a feeling of numbness in parts of my body at first. It could have been something simple but it persisted. In the back of my mind there was the fear that it might be this dreaded disease but I kept thinking and hoping that there would be some other explanation. Then came the proof - white patches on my skin. Just the size of a coin at first but soon growing to the size of my hand! I could not deny it any longer - but why me? I didn't deserve this! I railed against God and my parents - everyone! It just wasn't fair! Soon I wallowed in self-pity - what was to become of me? Finally I surrendered to the fact that I had leprosy and realised that for the sake of my family I should isolate myself from them to prevent the curse from spreading to the people I cared for so much!

I went to where the other lepers gathered and saw many who had been afflicted by the disease for much longer than I had. Shocking!! It was terrifying to see what probably lay ahead of me! The wasting of human flesh, the distortion of bone and cartilage crippling so many limbs - and some of the victims were quite young. The less disabled were helping those who were hardly able to help themselves. Was it from kindness I wondered? Perhaps they harboured the forlorn hope that, when their turn came, someone would show such kindness to them. I considered if it might not be more kind just to leave the severely disabled alone to die!

We had to stay well away from healthy people and if we came near to any normal person we had to tell them that we were "unclean".

Yes! Humiliation was piled on top of disability! What I missed most was my family - a warm hug, the feeling of my mothers arms around me and the love all of us shared. Now, when I saw them, it was at a distance and I could hardly bear to look into their eyes, for there I saw their despair at seeing my deterioration. I would return to the companionship of my fellow lepers with the resignation that this disease would take its toll.

I was from Samaria but most of the group of lepers came from Galilee and one day ten of us were at the border between the two countries when we saw Jesus. We had heard of the miracles He had performed and that He was passing this way. When we saw Him our instinct was to rush to Him and beg for healing but propriety kept us at a distance. We shouted so that He would be able to hear us: "Jesus, Master, take pity on us". Those who were with Him recoiled when they realised what we were but Jesus showed no sign of revulsion as He told us to go and show ourselves to the priests. This was the requirement for anyone who had been sick and had been cured as the priest could then declare that person "clean".

The meaning of His words slowly sank in and we started off in the direction of the priests. It was not a gradual improvement. One moment they were there - next moment the white patches were gone - so had the numbness! I stared and stared, checking and rechecking - it was true - I was healed! Not only did I have my health restored but I would have my family back! It felt like I had been given a new life. I could see that the other nine had been healed too as they hurried to be certified healthy by the priests.

Jesus was still standing there. I approached, threw myself at His feet and declared my undying gratitude. To be honest no words could possibly convey how I felt. Jesus noted that only one of the ten who had been healed had come to thank Him. The others, who were from His homeland, had not even thought of it while I, a foreigner to Him had done so. He told me that my faith had made me well!

As I held on to that faith I started to realise that it appeared to be the pattern for people in general to thank Him for only one out of every ten or so blessings He bestows. I try to ensure that pattern does not apply to me. How about you?

JAIRUS

Many of you will not have heard of me but I'm sure you will have heard of my daughter. I was a leader in a Synagogue by the side of Lake Galilee and my name is Jairus. One day, my daughter fell ill and, at first I thought that it was just one of those illnesses which she would throw off after a day or two. But no! She got worse and worse until my wife and I began to fear for her life.

The local doctors seemed unable to find a cure and finally my wife in desperation said that she had heard of a man called Jesus who was said to have healed many sick people and that He was in our area today. Why didn't I go to Him for help? I knew that the Chief Priest was condemning this man but I, myself was undecided about Him. If I approached Jesus for help, I risked that wrath of the Chief Priest but on the other hand my daughter desperately needed help! I just wasn't sure what was the right thing to do! I glanced at my daughter and immediately my mind was made up - she couldn't hold out much longer!

It wasn't difficult to find Jesus for there was a large crowd around Him. Normally I am not the kind of man who would cause a fuss but my daughter's life was at stake - I pushed through the crowd and got close to Jesus. I told Him that my daughter was dying - could He please come and heal her? How would He react? I looked into His face and saw such calm repose and yet I could sense a pent up power within this man! But more than that - above all else was the overwhelming impression of authority. He exuded honesty, integrity, assurance and purity. Instantly, I trusted Him.

When He agreed to come I felt for the first time in many days that all would be well. We started off for my home but He suddenly stopped and asked who had touched Him. It was a strange question for there were crowds all around Him but a woman came forward looking quite afraid and told Him that she had suffered from severe bleeding for years and nothing the doctors did had helped. She said she felt that if she could just touch His cloak she would be healed! Jesus smiled and put her at ease and you could actually feel the love that flowed from Him as He told her that her faith had made her well. Apparently she was completely cured!

My thoughts returned to my daughter and mentally I said "Oh, come on Jesus before it's too late" Just at that moment my heart sank as I saw some of my friends who had come from my house. My worst fears were realised when they, obviously in distress, told me that my little girl had died. "Let's not bother the teacher any more" they said. Strangely my spirits were once again lifted when Jesus told me to have faith and that everything would be alright.

When we arrived at my house the mourners were already weeping and wailing. My wife was distraught and said simply that we were too late our daughter was dead. When Jesus said she was just sleeping many people mocked Him - He took my wife, myself and three of His disciples into the room where my daughter was lying, took her hand and said "little girl - get up!" The chills ran down my spine as I saw her stir. Tears of gratitude and joy filled my eyes as she arose - restored to full health. Jesus told us to get her something to eat but we were so astounded that we could hardly move. This man who had power over death could be my Lord no matter what the Chief Priest would say. I was so overcome, hugging my daughter that I hardly even thanked Him.

Some time later, I couldn't believe it when I heard that He had been put to death. Was it true? This man who had power over death couldn't save Himself? It troubled me deeply and then I got it! He was the one the scriptures spoke about - the one who was to be rejected - the one God chose to be the saviour - He was the one who died to pay the price for sin! He was the Messiah!! Not only was He able to restore people to life physically but He could bring the spiritually dead to eternal life!.

Yes I will always remember Him for giving my daughter back her life and I will always bow my head in reverent gratitude for being given the opportunity to experience eternal life with Him in Heaven!

ZACCHAEUS

I hated being referred to as "little Zacchaeus" which was a constant reminder of my lack of stature. I wanted them all to treat me with respect and so when the opportunity presented itself to buy into the Roman system of tax collection I grabbed it with both hands. The Romans allocated to me an area and I was told how much tax to put into their coffers.

Of course, we tax collectors could add a bit to enable us to earn a living. In common with most others I added quite a sum for my own benefit and as a result became quite unpopular – but very rich! The enthusiasm I displayed in my job came to the attention of the authorities who appointed me to be a chief tax collector which made me even more unpopular, but even richer! The people knew they were being exploited but they could do little about it as we had the Roman Empire backing us. I didn't stay awake at night worrying about the predicament of the poor - served them right for calling me "little Zacchaeus". Now I had their overt respect even if I also had their hidden contempt.

Then one day I saw a large crowd of people and went to investigate. They were following a man called Jesus who was passing through my town of Jericho on His way to Jerusalem. Of course I had heard of Him - who hadn't with all the healing and dynamic preaching of God's word He was reported to have carried out. Could He really be the one to free the Jews from Roman oppression? Many people thought so!

I was curious about Him. What did He look like? The Pharisees seemed to decry Him and the message He proclaimed but the ordinary man in the street thought He was a prophet sent by God.

Here was an opportunity to see Him for myself and perhaps if luck was on my side hear Him preach.

Standing at the back of the crowd I wasn't tall enough to see very much so I ran ahead to a spot where a sycamore tree overhung the road. Climbing the tree was easy and I knew there would be a good view from that point.

The crowd came closer and then I saw Him! There was no evidence of His being a fierce warrior. No anger, no hate or vindictiveness and no wild exhortation to violence or rebellion in fact, He didn't look very different from the others except that He had a certain - well what can I call it? His bearing was regal, unhurried, and somehow commanded respect. He drew near, looked up at the tree, held my gaze and called my name. "Zacchaeus, hurry down" He said "I am going to stay at your house tonight". How did He know my name? Although I was by then a rich and influential man I felt strangely flattered that He had chosen me. Delighted, I climbed down and spoke to Him.

It was then that I felt His purity, innocence, power, insight, love............ Oh! a whole book could hardly contain what I felt. It was as if a light was shining in my soul showing me a glimpse of Heaven, but the same light also showed up the darkness of my own corruption - the way I had been harsh, greedy and unfair in collecting the taxes. Right there and then, I knew what I had to do. My riches were much more than I required - I would give half to the poor - and everyone I had treated unfairly would be recompensed.

My money, status, even my physical inadequacies no longer seemed important. I could see in His eyes that God loved me in spite of everything I had done!

When He confirmed my salvation I was certainly a different person - a new man - some might even say I had been born again.!!

PONTIUS PILATE

Pontius Pilate Procurator of Judea!! It had a nice ring to it. I repeated my title over and over and felt my heart swell with pride in my position. I had always been aware that my Roman superiors didn't have a great deal of confidence in me but here at last, was a position of real power and maybe a stepping stone to greater things.

Over the years there had been some difficult times when the Jews had caused me problems and I had been reprimanded by the Emperor but I still had my position and I intended to keep it and with some luck rise to a higher echelon. Of course I would have to be careful not to ruffle too many feathers but showing a firm hand was the way to win the respect of the people and of my superiors, or so I thought. The Jewish hordes thought of me as a harsh ruler but I believe I allowed some latitude from time to time.

There they were again annoying me with some trivial matter about their own religious laws. They told me that a man was claiming to be a king. What was his name? Jesus? When the Chief Priests brought Him before me I could see they were plainly jealous of Him for He had attracted quite a following although His followers had caused no trouble to the Roman Empire. Why couldn't they deal with this matter themselves? I just didn't have the appetite for this insignificance which these religious fanatics held in such high regard so when I heard that Jesus came from Galilee I saw an opportunity to get rid of this irritation. King Herod was responsible for that area and the people of Galilee. He could decide the matter.

Herod was pleased that I sent Jesus to him for judgement. I suppose he believed he was being honoured by me. We had never been close but after this we developed a friendship. However, he was unable to decide matters and gave the problem back to me.

I spoke to Jesus asking Him what this was all about and He answered by talking about the truth. Truth? What was a Jewish truth might be different to a Roman truth. I asked Him "What is truth?" He seemed reluctant to elaborate. When asked if the accusation of His being a king was true He replied that His kingdom was not of this world and so I saw no danger to the establishment.

When I told the Jewish crowd that I had found no reason to condemn this man the Chief Priests whipped them up to a frenzy and they responded by demanding His death by crucifixion. I could see He was innocent and things got worse when my wife hurried to tell me not to do Him any harm because she had had a dream which showed Him to be innocent and it disturbed her greatly.

The crowd by now was getting close to rioting! How would that look on my record? I could not afford to have my reputation tarnished in that way. My hopes of greater things would go up in smoke - even my position here in Judea would be in jeopardy. But He was innocent! That fact could not be denied! I tried different ways to spare His life. The Jewish Passover was immanent and as it was my custom at that time to free one of the prisoners, I offered Jesus - they demanded Barabbas who was an insurrectionist and a murderer! I had Jesus whipped - a punishment which brought many men close to death - it did not satisfy them!

They said that because He claimed to be a king He was the enemy of the Emperor. The threat was plain! Have Him crucified or the Emperor would hear about how I let a man who was seen to be his enemy go free! I couldn't afford that so against my will, I let them have their wish. Publicly I washed my hands to indicate that the vileness of this deed was not my doing and that it would leave no stain on my soul. A grand gesture but my soul was stained.

I had a notice prepared and placed on His cross stating that He was the king of the Jews. It was written in Hebrew, Latin and Greek because this upcoming Passover festival was a special one and people would be arriving in Jerusalem from all over the Empire. At least they would be able to read in their own language that Jesus was the king of the Jews.

With the passage of time He proved to be not only the king of the Jews but the world wide king of kings!!

BARABBAS

I was in prison awaiting execution for murder and insurrection when I heard my name being shouted by the crowds outside. "Barabbas! Barabbas!" they chanted in unison. I had no idea why. Did they want me to be handed over to them so that they could tear me limb from limb? That did not seem likely because many of them secretly supported the uprising. Perhaps they wanted me to be the first one to be crucified. I would just have to wait and see.

Sitting there in prison I had tried not to think of what lay ahead of me but the thoughts were too powerful and insistent and would not be subdued. Time and time again I considered what the executioners would do to me. The pain of the nails being driven through my hands and feet, the agony of being hoisted up on a cross! I knew that some unfortunate wretches had hung there for many hours, even days before death released them from the torture. I also knew that merely contemplating the pain came nowhere near to experiencing the agony that lay in front of me. The one good thing was that the Sabbath was next day and the Jewish authorities would want us dead before then so that they could remove our bodies from the crosses. Imagine my situation! To die quickly was all I could hope for!

Two others were to die with me for crimes which were perhaps less grave than mine but the Romans decreed that they deserved the same fate.

Still the chanting continued - what could it be? I couldn't quite hear the discussion which was taking place but I did recognise the voice of Pontius Pilate, the Roman procurator and occasionally the name of Jesus was mentioned. I had heard that Jesus was a good man. Some people even thought that He would be the leader who would win our country back from the Romans. Perhaps I should have asked Him to join our uprising.

Thoughts of the impending pain once again broke into my consciousness. There was no escape! My mind could hardly stand it! I was sweating with dread, shaking with fear! Then the crowd cheered!

Soon afterwards the gate opened and two guards marched into my cell and took hold of me! This is it I thought. They unfastened my chains and told me I was free to go! Pilate had been in the habit of releasing one prisoner at the Passover and as that festival was upon us the shouting crowd had chosen to free me but as I learned, Jesus was to take my place! I doubt if you can possibly understand my relief and joy. I hurried out of the place just in case they changed their minds and I hid among the crowd.

I could see from the way the flesh had been stripped from His back that Jesus had been severely whipped! Men had died from that punishment alone and Jesus, himself, had been greatly weakened. He was made to carry His own cross on the way to the place they called Golgotha but kept staggering under its weight and so the the Roman soldiers got someone from the crowd to carry it for Him.

I winced as the nails were driven into Him thinking it should have been me! I remembered the mental anguish I had suffered while contemplating the pain of being lifted up - nailed to a cross. It had not begun to convey this degree of agony.

From a distance I saw the other two who had been imprisoned with me, now crucified also, one on each side of Him. They appeared to be berating Him but as I drew closer I heard Him reassure one of them by saying that he would be in Paradise with Jesus that very day. It seemed an odd thing to say through pain. Was he trying to hold on to a little hope when all hope had gone? I don't know!

Later, I learned more about Jesus - about how He claimed to be the Son of God, of how He had healed many people, of His preaching and even how He had restored dead people to life. I realised that,in a sense, that was what He had done for me perhaps in a greater way than you can possibly understand!

MARY MAGDALENE

If I told you how terrible I had been you probably would not want to hear from Mary of Magdala. I said and did things any normal person would abhor. No one held out any hope for me - and after a while no one cared. No one except Jesus! I desperately wanted help - in my more sane moments anyway - but I had chased all my friends away. They couldn't deal with my irrational behaviour and deliberately avoided all contact with me. Inside, I was the same Mary as I had always been - honest and kind - but it seemed that someone or something had power over my actions and my body and my speech.

When I first met Jesus He looked deep inside me into the very essence of my being and saw the real me! He knew what I was suffering and I heard Him address me - no not me - He spoke to what was possessing me. He commanded my demons to depart from me. Seven evil spirits left my body never to return and I experienced a peace I had never known before! At last, free to be myself and perhaps more than myself, for I was also aware of a loving presence keeping me safe, I surrendered my life to this man I then knew to be the Son of God.

That was when I felt His love - a love which did not depend on what I had done or would do! It had no conditions attached! Unlike the other men I had known He wanted nothing in return! He loved me with a pure uncomplicated love just because I was me! It was easy to understand why so many people put their trust and faith in Him! From that moment on I loved Him in return and became one of His followers who helped with ordinary but necessary tasks which left Him free to do His Father's work - and I felt honoured to do so.

We were happy to feel that we were part of God's purpose, but then came the day He had warned us about - the whole reason for His coming to earth as a man - to pay the price for the sin of mankind! It meant, of course that He had to offer himself to fulfil the Law of sacrifice instituted through Moses. Every other sacrificial offering had been merely a shadow of this - the perfect sacrifice!

I know He had the power to prevent it but He chose to suffer humiliation, scourging and finally death on a cross in order to save all mankind from having to pay the penalty for sin. Several of us women watched the crucifixion, from a distance at first, with tears flowing down our cheeks. Later we were able to get closer and heard his final words. Even in His death throes, His great love was evident.

I was also there when they took His body down from the cross and placed it in a tomb given by a secret follower called Joseph who came from Arimathea. That was on the Friday. Saturday was the Sabbath when we were not permitted by Jewish law to do any work but as early as possible on Sunday morning I went, with two other women, to anoint His body with spices and herbs.

We were wondering how we would ever be able to move the large stone which sealed the tomb but as we approached, the ground trembled and I saw someone dressed in the whitest robes I had ever seen. It was an angel! He had rolled the stone away and the tomb was empty! Two Roman guards who had been posted there to keep watch on the tomb stood frozen to the spot! The angelic being told us not to be afraid for Jesus had risen from the dead! We hurried to tell the disciples. At first we were overcome with a mixture of fear and joy and could say nothing but then it all poured out. When they managed to unravel the cascade of words they were overjoyed but uncertain whether or not to believe what they were hearing.

A little later one of the most momentous events of my life took place. I was sitting at the tomb when two angels dressed in those dazzlingly white clothes appeared and then there was a third person. I didn't really look at Him until He said my name. It was Jesus! The Lord - resurrected!! Love and joy mingled in a confusion of emotions!

Now I know the Lord lives forever!! And He is my Saviour!! Hallelujah!

JOSEPH OF ARIMATHEA

Although I came from Arimathea, I was a member of the Jewish Council in Jerusalem which was called the Sanhedrin. My name is Joseph and I wanted to honour the beliefs and traditions of my ancestors but I could not deny that the teaching of a young man called Jesus seemed to strike a chord in me. I felt that nothing He said contradicted the Scriptures, instead He was able to throw some light on many of the difficult scripture passages. I examined His words and passed through various stages of belief in Him from, seeing that He was a good man, to respecting His intelligence, to recognising His wisdom, to regarding Him as a prophet, and finally to realising that He was the Son of God.

Most of the other Pharisees rejected Him without weighing the worth of His proclamations. They simply closed their minds to the insights His words contained. You may feel that perhaps, I should have left the Council but I felt that I stood a better chance of influencing their decisions from within rather than being seen as an opponent. So I tried to bring about change in a quiet, subtle manner while remaining a secret believer in Jesus Christ. Maybe that influence was not as effective as His teaching deserved but I did try.

To be honest, however, I was afraid of what they would do if the other members of the Sanhedrin discovered my new religious affinity. I suppose I ought to have been more conscientious in exercising faith just as Jesus was when He saw how the Temple area was being abused by merchants who were treating the forecourt like a market place! That was when He formed a whip from some cords and chased the animals and merchants from area. He told them that they had turned His father's house into a den for thieves!

Can you imagine anyone having the courage, strength, power and authority to do that? Well Jesus did! His image is projected by some as being so compassionate that He seems a bit soft and lily livered but make no mistake about it - Jesus was a man of immense power!

Of course, this incident depicted the strength of His love for the temple, His father's house, but at other times the strength of His love for the ordinary people was shown clearly. For example, He declared that not only should we love our friends and neighbours, but that we should also love our enemies and help them whenever we can! I know lots of people found difficulty with this teaching because they almost seemed to enjoy the anger and bitterness their enemies evoked but it was made clear that holding on to spite does more physical and mental harm to ourselves than to the person our spite is directed against.

And He told everyone to forgive others not just seven times but seventy times seven times meaning, of course, every time forgiveness is required. Yes! It is demanding being one of His followers but when He has your heart, you want to do these things to please Him.

There was one time in particular when His wisdom and compassion completely floored the teachers of the Law and the Pharisees. They brought before Him a woman who had been caught in the act of committing adultery and asked Him what should happened to her. It was a planned, perfidious, ploy to trap Jesus. You see, under the Law given by God to Moses, she should be stoned to death but we were in subjection to Roman authority and were not allowed to put anyone to death on our own. If Jesus said not to stone her He would be seen to be contradicting the sacred Law and His opponents would claim He was guilty of sacrilege. On the other hand, if He said they should uphold the law and stone her, He would be violating a Roman decree. Checkmate? Not for Jesus! He said that whoever had never sinned could cast the first stone. What a perfect response! Not even the most pious Pharisee would claim that! Slowly they all went away

163

leaving the woman alone with Jesus. He told her she could go on her way but that she should stop her sinful behaviour.

Many people tried to argue with Him but no one was a match for His intellect and He always showed concern for what each person really required. He saw behind the front they presented and spoke to their inner need. Nevertheless, when He declared that He was the bread of life, many people turned away from Him because they did not fully understand the meaning of what He said. I took it that He meant that by His words we would be nourished in a spiritual sense. Another difficult statement He made was that He was the light of the world! Quite simply, I believed this meant that enlightenment of His father's will was found in His teaching.

He performed miracle after miracle. Who but God's own son could do all that? Do you know that at one time He and His disciples were in a boat in the middle of a storm? The disciples believed they were about to drown and cried to Jesus for help. He told the wind and the waves to be still and immediately they were! Obviously God had granted Him power over everything. That is why it was so surprising when He was put to death on a cross. They claimed He was guilty of blasphemy. Wasn't it ironic that the son of God should be crucified because He said He was the son of God but of course, the Pharisees still had their minds closed!

When the dead bodies were being removed from the crosses I asked Pontius Pilate, the Roman procurator, if I could take Jesus' body and place it in the tomb I had built for myself. I was glad when he agreed for the thought of Jesus Christ being buried in a mass grave was abhorrent to me.

The grief I felt as He died was shared by many who had known His love and we walked around with our senses numb on Friday, the day of His death and all day Saturday, the Sabbath, but then came the most glorious Sunday I had ever known! Resurrection Sunday! Christ is risen! - Yes! He is risen indeed!

DOUBTING THOMAS

I ask you is it fair? I made a simple error in judgement on one occasion and I have been branded as Doubting Thomas all through the centuries! It happened like this:

There had been twelve of us disciples following and learning from the Master for a period of three years - now there were only eleven and the Master was dead. He had been crucified on the false charge of blasphemy simply because the Pharisees and the Chief priests were angry and jealous that He revealed the truth from the scriptures and was more popular than they were. On top of that, He had been betrayed by one of our own number, a man named Judas who had since killed himself because he could not live with the guilt of his treachery.

His crucifixion had been horrendous! Thankfully, He died after a few hours and in order to make sure He was dead one of the Roman soldiers rammed his spear into Jesus' side. We saw what looked like blood and water pour out which proved beyond doubt that He was no longer alive.

The other ten disciples had been meeting together but I had some other business to attend to and when I met up with them again they were positively aglow and talking excitedly! How could they expect me to believe what they were saying - that they had seen the Master alive?

What nonsense they seemed to be talking! I felt, at first that this was a joke they had decided to play on me but I quickly ruled that out, for all of us had been very depressed after His death. It was not the time for jokes! Maybe they had been so desperate to see Him again that they had had a mass hallucination. I had heard that kind of thing can happen, particularly when people are vulnerable and open to suggestion and we certainly qualified on that score.

Was I the only one holding on to his sanity? Had they all gone soft in the head? I felt I had to put them right and reasoned with them indicating that they should have examined His body closely because hallucinations don't have flesh and bones and told them that I would only believe what they said if I could put my fingers on the scars in His hands and my hand into the spear wound in his side. They became more fervent, trying to convince me but I just thought they were being hysterical which to my mind proved the hallucination theory! We would just have to agree to disagree!

However not long after, my thoughts were turned on their head. The eleven of us were together behind locked doors when suddenly, we were twelve! How did the other man get in? And, yes he looked like Jesus! It was Jesus!! He called my name and told me to put my fingers on His wounds and my hand in His side. I looked straight at Him and did not need to touch Him. Oh! how wrong I had been! They hadn't been joking nor hallucinating! I was embarrassed and ashamed because I realised that He knew what I had said to the ten.

Yes, I had doubted but my doubt was over what the others had said not about Jesus Himself! I bowed my head and confessed Him as "My Lord and my God!" because I knew without any doubt that He was God incarnate - that He had been put to death on a cross and was now resurrected never to die again! His reprimand to me was gentle as He said that I believed because I saw with my own eyes but how blessed were those who believed without seeing Him! This, I suppose, is what the Christian faith is all about. All the things He had said before His death fell into place. Things like that He was going to His father and that we would see Him again three days after He had been put to death. I could understand that the whole purpose of His earthly mission was to fulfil His father's will.

I worked hard to spread the message of salvation after that incident and know that many people believed because they felt an inner conviction and not because they were given the proof through their own eyes as I was

No matter how hard I try I suppose I will always be known as Doubting Thomas which, perhaps, is no bad thing for when a hard headed sceptic like me is convinced - then the gospel of Christ must be true

STEPHEN

After Jesus died and the apostles had been filled with the Holy Spirit, the number of believers continued to grow in Jerusalem and many in our ranks were happy to sell their property in order to contribute to the common purse. Money was distributed according to the need of each individual and everyone regarded the others as members of one big family - brothers and sisters of Jesus Christ Himself. Many Jewish priests were converted to our faith and God blessed the movement with joy and love.

Some time later, however, the Greek-speaking Jews brought to Peter's attention the fact that the widows in their number were not receiving a fair share of the daily allocation of funds. The apostles asked the members of our order to appoint seven men to supervise the distribution of finances. Apparently most people thought very highly of me and along with six others I, Stephen, was voted on to the team which oversaw the apportioning of the money.

The Holy Spirit worked His power in me enabling me to perform miracles and to spread the faith by my example of loving Christian living. So much so that my actions came to the attention of some non-believing Jews who tried to confront me with their arguments. No matter how hard they tried, they could not discredit the Way of the Lord and decided to bring false charges against me. They claimed that I had insulted the Temple, undermined the Law of Moses and tried to alter the customs of our ancestors. None of these things was true, of course, but I was brought before the Sanhedrin and questioned.

I decided to show my respect for the traditions of my Jewish upbringing and talked about the great Patriarchs of the Jews. I described how Abraham had been told by God to leave the place where he was living and go to Haran and later to the promised land where we now lived. God said that this land would one day belong to his descendants although at the time Abraham had no children. I gave them an account of our history by saying that Abraham's descendants travelled to Egypt where they became slaves for four hundred years. But they were blessed by God who enabled them to leave Egypt to live in the land of Canaan. As a sign of His covenant, God gave Abraham the rite of circumcision and when his son Isaac was born the boy was circumcised when he was eight days old. Isaac did the same to his son Jacob and Jacob did likewise to all twelve of his sons whose descendants were the twelve tribes of Israel. The other sons of Jacob became angry and jealous of their brother Joseph, his father's favourite, and sold him to a band of Midianite traders who, in turn, sold Joseph into slavery in Egypt. Joseph earned respect and pleased the king by revealing the meaning of a dream. He was rewarded by being made the most important man in Egypt under the king. When a seven year long famine hit the land Jacob sent ten of his other sons to Egypt to buy corn from Joseph. When the famine continued a second journey to Egypt was necessary and on this occasion Joseph let them know he was their brother and invited them to come and live with him in Egypt where they would be given the best of land to live on. All seventy-five members of the family accepted the invitation. The numbers of our ancestors grew greatly but as the years passed and Joseph was forgotten, our people were treated like slaves. Then Moses was born at a time when it had been decreed that all male children born to the Israelites were to be killed. In a desperate attempt to save his life, Moses was put in a basket and placed in the river Nile where he was found by the princess who brought him up in the Egyptian palace. As an adult he defended one of the Israelite slaves from harsh treatment from a guard and ended up killing the Egyptian. Moses beat a hasty retreat to the land of Midian where he settled, until God spoke to him from a burning bush telling him to lead God's people out of Egypt. After a series of miracles, Moses was able to lead the Israelites into the wilderness where he was given the Ten Commandments. Later, Joshua invaded and conquered the land of Canaan and our ancestors settled there until the time of king David who was another great man of God. His son Solomon was the one who built the Temple!

I looked around at the faces of my jury and saw that they were impressed. There was nothing they could disagree with in what I had said. Then I hit them right between the eyes! I told them they were stubborn; that they had always ignored the Holy Spirit and that just like their forebears they put to death the prophet of God! Their countenance changed as I saw the darkness of anger drift across their countenances but then I had a vision of the Glory of God and told the members of the Sanhedrin that I could see Heaven open up and Jesus sitting at the right side of the Father! Furious, they dragged me out to stone me to death! As the first stone struck me I fell to my knees and cried out to God "Don't hold this sin against them!"

Even at my death I was able to witness for the Lord, for as the life was pounded out of me I noticed a young man holding the cloaks of those who were throwing the stones. Our eyes met and he saw no anger, hate or despair in me - only love! There was surprise in his expression! He became known as Paul, one of the greatest ambassadors for the Lord which the world has ever seen!

PHILIP

Sometimes people mistake me for the apostle, because we are both called Philip, but I was not privileged to be as close as that to Jesus when He was alive. From the time of my conversion, however, He has been in my heart and mind and I have been guided by the Holy Spirit ever since I put my faith in Him.

Along with Stephen and five others, I helped to administer the distribution of funds to the needy poor in our group of believers. Our undertaking this responsibility, meant that the apostles were freed to spend their time preaching the good news that Jesus saves anyone who accepts Him as Lord and Saviour. We, also, had time to engage in evangelism ourselves and did so with relish but I was shocked, as we all were, to hear that Stephen had been stoned to death, having been convicted on a false charge of blasphemy, as Jesus had before him. After his death, the persecution really started and many believers were scattered all over the country. The intention was to stamp out this "new Way" but it had the opposite effect as wherever they ended up our brothers and sisters spoke of the gospel of Jesus Christ and little communities of faith sprang up all over the land.

Personally, I went to a city in Samaria and preached to a crowd there about the Lord. They listened attentively and were amazed when, by the Spirit's power, I drove out demons from those who were possessed, healed the lame and cured many who were paralysed. They were excited and joyful as they became aware of the truthfulness of the message and witnessed Christ's power in action. A great number were baptised into the Way of Christ, including a man named Simon who had been highly regarded by the Samaritans because he appeared able to perform all kinds of magic. However, they had never seen anything like the supernatural power of the Spirit of Christ. After his baptism Simon stayed close to me, hoping to discover the "trick" to it.

The apostles, Peter and John, heard about the great conversion taking place in Samaria and came from Jerusalem to see the developments for themselves. They were delighted with the results and prayed that those who believed, would be given the Holy Spirit. As they laid hands on each person, so that man or woman received the Spirit.

Simon saw all this and wanted to have the gift of bestowing the Spirit upon people himself and so he offered money to Peter and John asking them to give him that power. Peter chastised him; told him that his motives were all wrong, that he should repent of the evil of his thoughts and get rid of the envy which was making him a captive to sinful behaviour. Simon was stunned but still had the presence of mind to ask Peter and John to pray for his forgiveness.

The two apostles returned to Jerusalem, preaching in each Samaritan city they journeyed through on the way. I also left Samaria as the Lord had work for me to do elsewhere. I was told to go south to the road from Jerusalem to Gaza which, of course, I did. As I was travelling along this road, I spotted a chariot and immediately heard the voice of God telling me to go to the chariot and stay close to it. I saw that there was an Ethiopian inside and heard him read scripture from the prophet Isaiah. It was the part where the death of the Saviour was prophesied. I asked him if he understood what he was reading and he replied that he wished someone would explain it to him. I was invited into the chariot and discovered that he was an important official in Ethiopia. Starting with the scripture he had been reading, I explained about Jesus Christ and as I did he kept nodding his head in agreement and acceptance. He felt God calling him to dedicate his life to Jesus and when we came to a stretch of water he asked me to baptise him! We both went into the water and he was baptised! What joy shone from his face! I wondered what impact he would have on his return to Ethiopia! Later I found out and was not disappointed!

The Holy Spirit took me to Azotus and I travelled on to Caesarea preaching Jesus in every town I came to. I settled in Caesarea and was blessed in that I had four lovely daughters each of whom preached the message with great eloquence and when I played host to Paul on one of his journeys he was impressed by my "girls". I felt that God had truly smiled on us and it occurred to me that although God is concerned with the big picture, He doesn't overlook the smallest detail in our lives!

CORNELIUS

The Roman army was an all-conquering fighting machine which captured and occupied land after land making the people subject to the Emperor in Rome and I was proud to be part of it. Nevertheless, I had a certain sympathy with the Jews in Judea. My name is Cornelius and I had made a study of Jewish scripture and respected their traditions as far as my position as Centurion in the Roman army would allow. In fact, the more I learned about the God of Israel, the more I realised that the gods worshipped in the Roman Empire were false. It gave me a dilemma, however. How could I worship Almighty God and at the same time serve the Emperor? The words that Jesus was reported to have said came to my aid: "Give to Caesar what is Caesar's and to God what is God's!"

This put things in perspective and when I heard that Peter had told the Jewish Council that we must put what God tells us to do before the instructions from man, I knew I could function under the Emperor as long as I was not asked to do anything which violated God's commands. It was on that basis that I performed my duties while learning to worship God. Indeed my whole family saw the truth and joined me in praying to the Lord.

It was my pleasure to be able to help the poorer of the Jews for I was a wealthy man with many servants. One day in mid-afternoon I had a vision! Surprisingly, I felt no fear! An angel said to me that my actions had won God's approval and that I should send some men to Peter in Joppa and ask him to come to see me. I did as he said and the servants who were sent to Joppa told me later that as they neared their destination Peter, himself, had a vision where he saw the gates of Heaven open and a large sheet descended to earth - inside, it held all kinds of animals. The voice of God told Peter to kill and eat the

174

animals. Peter said that he could not consume any animal which was "unclean" but the voice told him that nothing was unclean which the Lord declared to be clean. This procedure occurred three times and left Peter struggling to understand its significance. As he pondered on this matter, he heard the Spirit's voice once again. This time he was told that three men were looking for him and that he should not hesitate to go with them.

My servants approached Peter who confirmed that he was, indeed, Peter the man they sought. They informed him that their master was a Centurion who worshipped God and was highly regarded by all the Jews in his area and that an angel from God had told him to invite Peter to his house so that his questions could be answered. Peter encouraged them to spend the night there and next morning they set off accompanied by some of the other believers.

In anticipation of their arrival I had arranged for several relatives and friends to come along to hear from this great man of God. As soon as I saw Peter I knelt at his feet. Imagine it - me a Centurion humbling myself in front of someone who was in subjection to me! But it was a spontaneous gesture in recognition of the fact that he was an officer in God's army and therefore, in a sense, he out-ranked me! Peter told me to stand up for he was only a man! I let him know of my angelic visitation and that I had requested him to visit me in obedience to God's word. In a very short time Peter recognised my standing as regards my faith in God and, realising that I was a Gentile (that is a non-Jew), the meaning of his vision became clear. He was being told that God accepted not only Jews but also the Gentiles through the sacrifice of Jesus Christ. He went on to tell me about how John the Baptist had prepared the way for Jesus and that Jesus displayed the power of God as He drove out demons and healed the sick. Peter continued, telling me about the teaching and parables of Jesus; how He had been falsely accused and put to death but, three days later, had been raised to life in a resurrected body; that He commanded his people to preach the message of salvation; that all of this had been foretold in the Jewish scriptures and that everyone who believed on

Him would have his sins forgiven through the atonement achieved on the cross.

At the end of this discourse I suddenly felt a strange fire inside me and soon discovered that the power of the Holy spirit had been poured out on me and on everyone present who had heard and believed Peter's message. It was a shock to Peter to see this happen as he had never expected to see the power of God's Spirit being given to anyone other than those of Jewish descent. However, he arranged for us to be baptised and reported to his brothers in Christ, back in Jerusalem, this new innovation from God.

That marked a turning point in the apostles' understanding of the universal nature of God's grace for it was the first recorded incidence of the Holy Spirit being bestowed upon a Gentile but it was far from the last!

PAUL

I was born of Jewish parents who lived in Tarsus and named me Saul but many years later an incident in my life caused my name to be changed to Paul which I thought was more appropriate as in Latin Paul signifies something of little value. My childhood was typically Jewish and I was naturally enthusiastic about my faith. In fact as a young man I went to Jerusalem to study under a great teacher named Gamaliel. I became a most zealous Pharisee. Prior to that I had learned the trade of tent-maker in my home town of Tarsus - the foremost town in Cilicia. I also learned to speak different languages and had the added advantage of being a Roman citizen - inherited from my father who had that distinction.

Living in Tarsus, I had been exposed to Jewish, Roman and Greek philosophies and cultures and so had a wide general knowledge. My natural zeal made me a devout Jew and I defended my faith vigorously. When I learned that many people were becoming followers of someone called Jesus, I condemned them. Even when a man named Stephen, one of the followers of this "new way", was brought to trial by the Jewish council, called the Sanhedrin, I was in favour of their verdict - the death sentence for blasphemy! Stephen was stoned to death and if I hadn't been holding the coats I would have joined those who stoned him. There was one thing, however, which made a lasting impression on me - Stephen in his last moments did not look like a villain in fact he looked like an angel and his final words were not in anger or hate for as he prayed I heard him ask his God not to hold "our sin" against us.

As this new movement started to spread I got authority from the Sanhedrin to search for those people, later called Christians, and to bring them to justice which I did with a vengeance. I would ask for letters of introduction to synagogues in different towns so that I could weed out the so called followers of the Lord and have them sent to Jerusalem for sentencing.

It was on one such project, going to Damascus, that things changed for me! A group of us were on the road when suddenly a light shone round me. I fell to the ground and someone said " Why are you persecuting me?" He said he was Jesus - but Jesus had been crucified; he was dead!! He told me to go to the city. I did not dare refuse for when the light went away I found I was blind. I stayed in the city for three days not eating or drinking. Then a man named Ananias came to me saying he had been sent by the Lord Jesus so that I might be able to see again and be filled with the Holy Spirit! At that very moment something was released from my eyes and I could see once again. Right away I was baptised and knew what it was like to be filled with the Holy Spirit! I saw clearly that Jesus was indeed the Holy Messiah! That was when I dedicated my life to Him.

In the light of Christ it became evident that the Pharisees had become bound by a mass of petty rules. They had added man-made laws to God's commandments to such an extent that the Spirit had been lost and they were in danger of worshipping their own ordinances. Jesus was quite different! He tore down the hypocrisy of self-righteous precepts and moved straight to the Spirit of the Law. In Him I felt doubly free! Firstly, by His simple teaching I was free from the chains of a multitude of binding and oppressive rules which hindered spiritual development and secondly, by His sacrifice I was free from the penalty which my sins would otherwise have earned me. I acknowledged and repented of the sins in my life, prayed for forgiveness and accepted Jesus as Lord of my life and Saviour of my soul. So great was the joy I experienced that I wanted to share it with everyone. The apostles, however, were suspicious of my motives at first but when they saw the love shining from my face they soon accepted that mine had been a true conversion.

I looked back at how I had persecuted the Lord's people and was ashamed but I was also certain of His forgiveness. It was then that my name was changed. From then on I learned everything I could from scripture, from His disciples and from the Lord Himself. I was surprised how His birth, life and death fulfilled the Jewish scriptures about the Messiah! Why had I not realised it before? I suppose it was not just my physical eyes He opened.

For the rest of my life I travelled all over the known world establishing churches wherever the Holy Spirit dictated. Don't think it was easy for I suffered imprisonment, beatings, whippings, shipwreck, stoning, betrayal and much more but I consider it all worthwhile for the love of my Saviour, Christ Jesus the Son of the most high God!

May His Grace be with you all!!

TIMOTHY

I don't think I can tell you the exact time I became a Christian. You see it seems that it was almost born into me but I do remember the time I consciously confirmed my faith and felt the power of the Holy Spirit stir me into life. It was the start of a joyous and exciting lifetime adventure. My name is Timothy and I considered myself to be Jewish - but a Jewish Christian! Both my mother Eunice and my grandmother Lois were devout Jews who had accepted the teachings of Jesus Christ and had brought me up in that faith. My father, however, was Greek and saw no benefit in having me circumcised as a child, as was the Jewish practice ,but in spite of this omission I considered myself to be a very real part of the Jewish tradition.

Never the most robust of children I, in fact, was quite delicate and became rather sensitive perhaps, some people might say, introspective. Nevertheless, I was noticed for my devotion to the faith and as a young man was recommended to a travelling preacher named Paul. My introduction to this great man was embarrassing because I was spoken of in the most glowing terms with words such as: devoted; honest; pure; absolutely trustworthy and so on sprinkling the report. My timidity and frequent ill health were not mentioned.

Meeting Paul was mind-blowing! His energy was beyond human understanding. You felt that no matter what the opposition, he would not be defeated. Complete assurance of the truthfulness of his faith oozed from every pore. Each and every action had an authority which came from a divine source and yet he was a pleasure to be with. I listened to him - awestruck - feeling joy deep inside me when he spoke of the Saviour and acknowledged the truth of his words as he said that we could not rely on earning our way into Heaven but had to be washed clean in the blood of Christ to be free from the stain of our sins. The Old Testament prophet, Jeremiah, put my feelings into words when he said that God's word burned like a fire in his heart. So it was with me and I was filled with the desire to share the good news about Jesus Christ.

Paul took me under his wing and became not only the great mentor of my faith but my spiritual father as well. Gradually he coaxed me out of my self-consciousness and helped me spread the Gospel message myself.

Over the years I accompanied Paul on some of his missionary journeys learning all the time, feeling my faith grow stronger. However, it was not all plain sailing as there were times of great persecution and Paul took the brunt of that but he seemed to feel honoured to be considered worthy to suffer for the spreading of the Word.

On one occasion he told me we would be preaching to other Jewish men and women and that these people would be more likely to accept me if they felt that I was completely Jewish. I knew he was talking about circumcision for until then I would say that I was Jewish but..... He told me that from a Christian point of view it was not necessary but for the sake of the others it might be better. The people in the area we intended to evangelise knew my father was Greek so in order to forestall any unnecessary opposition I agreed, with apprehension, to be circumcised. I was in pain for a few days and tender for weeks but I felt that I was now truly a Jewish Christian!

At another time, Paul felt I was spiritually mature enough to stay in Macedonia and continue to build the church there while he moved on. I must admit that I wept openly when we parted company and Paul, strong man though he was, also had to fight back the tears. He wrote to me occasionally and it was a joy to receive his letters - they always had the right advice and support just when I needed them most and as time passed I could detect no diminishing of the flame of his faith! When he asked me to visit him in Athens I was happy to do so to tell him of our progress and he was delighted to see me. We met again in Corinth and later in Ephesus where I worked to strengthen the group of believers which Paul had established.

I had been put in prison for preaching the Gospel of Christ but was released after a short time. Paul had been imprisoned more than once for the same reason. When I went to see him the last time he was in prison I was sad to learn that he felt his life was soon to end! But what a life it was!! A living Faith! My memorial to him would be:-

" He was a man who thought nothing of hardships because his eyes were always on the Lord Jesus!!"

BARNABAS

I was a Levite who lived in Cyprus and was originally named Joseph but when I became a Christian and the Apostles got to know me, they changed my name to Barnabas which they thought was appropriate as Barnabas means "one who encourages." I was pleased that they thought of me in that light.

Before going to Jerusalem I sold a field which I owned and brought the money to the apostles who described me as being full of the Holy Spirit and a man of great faith. It became my great desire to live up to their opinion.

In the early days of the church a man called Saul who was a Pharisee tried to eradicate the Christian movement by getting written permission from the High Priest to enter the temple and synagogues in every town in order to search out Christians and have them thrown into prison. He was singularly successful in his endeavours. However, on a trip to Damascus, he had a personal encounter with Christ, was made blind for three days, after which he did a complete about turn, acknowledged that Jesus was the Messiah and preached so powerfully in Damascus that many people turned to Jesus. He later changed his name to Paul. Saul means 'asked of God' while Paul means ' humbled or of little value' He went to Jerusalem to join the brotherhood of the disciples but the apostles were very wary of the man who had tried to destroy their faith, and so they rejected him believing that he was trying to infiltrate the movement in order to determine who the leaders were so that he could have them thrown into prison. I was aware of Paul's mighty conversion and preaching and so I vouched for his sincerity and faith, as a result of which, he was accepted into the fellowship of the church.

Some time later I was sent to Antioch to preach the message so I searched for Paul and brought him with me. We preached there for a year with great success and it was in Antioch that the believers were first called Christians.

We went on missions together and on one occasion went to a place called Lystra where Paul healed a man who had been lame from birth. The locals believed that we were Gods come down to earth and they named me Zeus and Paul, Hermes. Zeus was the god to whom they had built a temple and Hermes was his messenger and, in some traditions, the son of Zeus. They brought bulls and flowers to worship us and give us their devotion. We of course were affronted and told them to stop, explaining that we were only men like them but the message of Christ and salvation was explained in detail to them.

On another mission we took along a young man and cousin of mine, named Mark but unfortunately he called off before the end so when Paul and I were planning a further mission I thought that we should give Mark another chance but Paul refused saying that we could only take fully committed believers and as Mark had let us down before we could not risk being let down again. I believed that we should not hold his previous indiscretion against him and that we should give him a second chance. The disagreement became quite heated and so we decided to split up and Paul took a man called Silas and went to Syria while I took Mark and went to Cyprus. In a way it was a good move as we were then preaching the Gospel in two places at one time rather than just the one.

In the end Paul seemed to indicate that he had been wrong about Mark as in writing to Timothy while in prison he asked for Timothy to bring Mark with him as he, Mark, had been a great help. If Paul had had his way Mark might have felt rejected and drifted away from faith in Christ but being strengthened by our mission Mark grew in faith to the point where he wrote and gave us the Gospel of Mark which is in our Bibles today.

GOD"S WORD REVISITED - PART THREE.

SOME REVEALING THOUGHTS.

SUBJECT	PAGE NUMBER
1. How can God be so cruel?	187.
2. Is Jesus the only way?	190.
3. Why have you abandoned me?	195.
4 .Adam and Eve - fact or fable?	199.
5. Father or Mother God?	203.
6. The homosexual question.	205.
7. Judge not?	210.
8. Our awesome God.	213.
9. Corruption.	218.
10. Spiritual refreshment through cancer.	225.
11. The Old Testament in a nutshell.	228.
12. Jehovah's Witnesses fallacies.	239.
13. Why was Jesus baptised?	242.
14. We are the luckiest people.	244.

15. Who wrote the book of Hebrews?   251.

16. Melchizedek – a man of mystery.   253.

17. Threefold denial – threefold confession.   255.

18. Lukewarm faith   257.

"HOW CAN GOD BE SO CRUEL?"

"How can God be so cruel?" That was the statement made by a well known host of a television program recently. It wasn't really a question more of a declaration that no one can believe in a God who would create the cruelty we see in the world. This man was telling about two insects where one attacks and takes the other one captive paralysing it in the process. The victor then plants eggs into the body of the helpless insect. As the eggs hatch the grubs feed off the body of the living host. Therefore this man declares that as a loving God would not introduce this torture in any animal, a loving God cannot exist and that this barbaric behaviour is merely and solely a result of random evolution.

This man is credited with high intelligence but in trying to deny the existence of a loving God he chooses to overlook the fact that there is a great force of evil at work in the world. The architect of that evil is the devil who opposes every good purpose of God and is the source of the cruelty he describes. God's creation was perfect, lovely and good but the devil has endeavoured to corrupt the good things God has given even during the process of evolution. The cruelty does not come from God but from the force of evil who delights in debasing beauty.

Satanic depravity is not confined to insects as is evidenced throughout all stages of life right up to and including human beings. Nor is it confined to life. Just think of the internet. What a wonderful source of information and communication it is but it is corrupted by such things as pornography and cyber bullying. Just another example of the devil's cunning attempt to thwart the purposes and cast doubt on the goodness and even the existence of God.

I question the reputedly high IQ of this man who suggests that God does not exist. Undoubtedly he is a person of great knowledge but perhaps the influence of the evil one on his thinking curtails his ability to see the real possibility that a beautiful creation is being corrupted by the force of evil. Instead of stubbornly disbelieving in a good God, he should open up his mind to the realisation of the existence of an opposing force of evil and be careful not to submit to that influence for in trying to discredit God he is doing the devil's work.

However the question "Why does God allow bad things to happen?" cannot be ignored. If He is truly almighty and all-loving why doesn't God put an end to evil? Author David Pawson in his book "God and the gospel of Righteousness" suggests that either God is not almighty or that He is not all-loving and as the Bible clearly shows that He is indeed almighty it means that He cannot be all-loving and so the evil we see all around us must be in accordance with His will. But could there be another explanation? Here is a possibility.

In the early chapters of the book of Job we are told that there was a meeting in heaven where the heavenly beings, including Satan, who at that time was a powerful angel, presented themselves before God. When God pointed to Job and declared him to be the most righteous man on earth Satan replied that Job only worshipped God because he had great riches and a wonderful family and that if he, Satan, were allowed to attack Job, his worship would turn to cursing. On two occasions God agreed to give Satan permission to deal with Job in the way he chose which saw Job left without family, without riches and without health but Job stayed faithful to God and Satan was proved wrong. Having defeated Satan in this way God then restored Job to good heath and bestowed upon him twice the level of riches he had lost and gave him the same number of children as he had had before.

It is eminently possible that at the time of the garden of Eden another such meeting of heavenly beings took place where Satan entered into a agreement with God by saying that as God had made Adam and Eve perfect they would be unlikely to sin and so if he could make them sin, God should allow him to have the freedom to exercise his power over the earth. Well we know that Satan did succeed in making Adam and Eve sin and so God, in honouring His code of conduct, kept His word and agreed to allow Satan freedom to exercise his power on earth. It would appear that the agreement is still in force as we witness atrocities taking place all over the world and people dying of starvation

However, if Satan had been allowed complete freedom to do whatever he wanted how much worse this world would be. There would be no compassion, no joy, no truth. Everyone would be out for themselves and would ride roughshod over everyone else with no care or consideration for the harm they do or the hurts they inflict. The world would be full of hate, lies, selfishness, there would be no love and everyone would be bound for Hell ......if Satan had his way. But there is love in the world and people do care for each other which reveals that although God is bound to keep His side of the agreement, to allow Satan some freedom, He does prevent Satan from having his way completely. When we get to heaven we may be surprised to learn just how often God has taken action to curb Satan's activities and although bad things are allowed to happen God stops even worse calamities from happening here on planet earth.

It is possible then that all those bad things that God is allowing to happen are because He is still honouring the agreement made in the garden of Eden but one thing is certain: that one day, when Christ returns, all wrongs will be put right and Satan and his influence will be banished for eternity from the new heaven and earth.

IS JESUS THE ONLY WAY?

The question "Is Jesus the only way to salvation?" must be faced by every Christian in every congregation in the country as it is fundamental to the Gospel and gives rise to the underlying question - " Is the Bible the inspired word of God as is claimed in 2 Tim. 3:15/16?"

A plethora of scriptures strongly indicates that faith in Christ is the only way to salvation and yet if God is a loving God, full of grace, how can He consign anyone to hell?

It sounds arrogant of Christians to say that only those who come to Christ can enter the Kingdom of heaven and while there are 2.1 billion Christians in the world, there are also 1.5 billion people who follow Islam, 900 million Hindus, 400 million who follow Chinese religions, 370 million Buddhists and 14 million Jews. We know God to be a God of compassion and mercy and so how can He consign to hell those who devoutly try to live up to the good standards required by other faiths? What happens to the kindly old woman who never does anyone any harm and tries to live a good life but has not got around to accepting Christ? Would a compassionate God close the gates of heaven in their faces? What about those who have never heard of Christ – will they be condemned? Aren't all religions merely different roads to the same destination?

Firstly, the viewpoint of well respected evangelists such as Dr Billy Graham is adequately borne out in passages such as :-

Gal. 5:4. Those of you who try to be put right with God by obeying the law have cut yourselves off from Christ.

John 14:6. I am the way, the truth and the life, no one goes to the Father except by me.

Acts 4:12. Salvation is to be found through Him alone.

Gal. 2:21. I refuse to reject the grace of God. But if a person is put right with God through the law it means that Christ died for nothing.

Rom. 3:20. For no one is put right in God's sight by doing what the law requires

Eph. 2: 8/9. For it is by God's grace you have been saved through faith. It is not the result of your own efforts, but God's gift so that no one can boast about it.

Rom. 3: 25. God offered Him so that by His sacrificial death He should become the means by which people's sins are forgiven through their faith in Him.

There are many others which state that salvation is through faith in Jesus alone. If the word of God is as clear as that, why then is there a dispute? Well let us go a little further.

John 5:24 states "I am telling you the truth: whoever hear my word and believes on Him who sent me has eternal life, he will not be judged but has already passed from death to life."

John 3:18. "Whoever believes in the Son is not judged; but whoever does not believe has already been judged, because he has not believed in God's only Son."

The latter passage is referring to those who have had the opportunity to accept Jesus but have made the conscious decision not to do so. Therefore non-belief in this case implies rejection.

In effect the two passages above are saying that judgement has already taken place on those who accept Jesus as Lord and Saviour and on those who reject him. But there is another passage which we must examine in conjunction with all of the above scriptures.

John 5:28-30. The time is coming when all the dead will hear his voice and come out of their graves; those who have done good will rise and live, and those who have done evil will rise and be condemned.....I judge only as God tells me so my judgement is right.

Note that it says "all the dead" will be raised at this judgement. If judgement has already taken place on those who believe and on those who reject, who are being judged in this passage? Everyone else? There are three ways in which to understand this scripture -

1. It is the time when judgement comes into effect..

2. It is the judgement for the reward.

3. It is the judgement on all those who have neither accepted nor rejected Christ.

In fact the truth is probably that all three are correct and the answer to questions such as - what happens to the kindly old woman and the sincere devotee of a non Christian faith and those who have never heard of Christ is plain – they will be judged. How then will this judgement work? The Bible tells us how in John 3: 19-21 which says

"This is how the judgement works.; the light has come into the world, but people love the darkness rather than the light, because their deeds are evil. Anyone who does evil things hates the light and will not come to the light, because he does not want his evil deeds to be shown up. But whoever does what is true comes to the light in order that the light may show that what he did was in obedience to God."

Take the illustration of the pot-holer who having been underground in darkness for days, emerges to be confronted by the brilliance of the mid-day sunlight. His eyes would hurt so much that he would choose to scurry back into the darkness because of his discomfort in the light. Non-believers who have lived according to the power of darkness will choose to dwell in the darkness rather than approach the all consuming light of Christ, while those who have lived according to the light which has been revealed to them will be attracted to that same light of Christ. In a very real sense then non-believers choose their own fate. Therefore the answer to the question "how can a loving God consign anyone to hell?" is that He doesn't. God has established Christ as judge of all the earth in that He is the means of judgement but hell bound souls choose their final destination because they find the purifying light of Christ intolerable.

But if all good living non-believers are attracted to the light of Christ does this mean that the sacrifice of Christ was for no purpose? Of course not, because no sinned stained soul will be present in heaven and as everyone has sinned – see 1 John 1:10- we must all be washed clean by the saviour's blood.

Different religions may be considered as different roads to the same goal only in the sense that many roads lead to, say Wembley stadium, but that is where this concession ends because there is only one gate into heaven and that is flooded by the light of Christ. Only those who love the light will pass through that gate and be washed clean from the contamination of sin.

Imagine the greatest human love the world has ever seem and multiply it by infinity and you begin to understand the depth of the Father's love for his son. Yet it was that son he sent to die a torturous death on the cross to pay the price for our sins. If there had been any other way into heaven would God have asked this of his son? No, Jesus did not die simply to give us yet another entry into the catalogue of human religions. It is as He said - "No one goes to the Father except by me".

As Jesus has established the means of salvation right here and now, just as we are, what fools we would be to choose to rely on our own righteousness at the judgement seat, rather than to surrender to His call at this very moment.

Having survived nearly 2000 years of onslaught by the powers of evil the scriptures must surely be the inspired word of God and that word clearly states that Jesus is the only way.

<u>WHY HAVE YOU ABANDONED ME?</u>

<u>Read:</u> Psalm 22 and Hebrews 4: 12-16

God works in mysterious ways, in the world at large but also in personal lives. Sometimes it is difficult to understand, maybe even impossible until His loving care and desire for our growth and well-being are acknowledged.

When parents are teaching a child to ride a bicycle they are careful to hold on to the bike, making sure it doesn't topple over and making sure their child does not get hurt. They provide the helmet and elbow and knee protectors in case of a fall. They walk alongside the child steadying the machine as he or she tries to keep their balance. Eventually the child takes off and rides away on his/her own while the parent releases the bike and looks on with anxious pride. As he or she makes progress the child gains confidence and is able to control the bike themselves, enabling them, in time to negotiate traffic. If they ever get into difficulties they may wish their parent was still with them. But in a sense the parent is always with them as they remember the instructions and warning about safety that had been drilled into them. Later as the child grows up the parent may decide to take a hand in the next stage – teaching the now adolescent to drive.

Perhaps this is what God does for us. When we come to accept the Lord as our Saviour, He stays with us and watches over us carefully, helping and guiding us through the early stages of faith. Then when the time is right He expects us to use our own abilities to grow into whatever talents He has given us. If God were to do everything for us it would not enable us to grow, so sometimes He steps back to allow us to progress in our walk of Christian faith. At times like that it may seem that He has deserted us but when this happens it's either for our own good or the benefit of the world at large. It seems to be the way God works...... and after a period of apparent withdrawal, just like the aforementioned parent, God gets us ready for the next stage.

The feeling of being abandoned happened to the great heroes of the Bible too. Take Abraham when it seemed that his wife, Sarah could not have children; or Joseph when he was sold into slavery in Egypt; or Moses when the people rebelled against him and David when his son Absalom tried to take the throne from him........

Yes each of them may have believed that God had abandoned them at times but with the advantage of hindsight they would come to realise that God never completely abandons His children. When it appears that way, He is simply allowing us to grow in our own right or enabling us to be groomed for the next stage in the way ahead.

In Psalm22 David cries out "Why have you abandoned me?...." the same words which Jesus cried out from the cross. Have you ever felt forsaken like that? It's bad enough when friends and family desert you but when even God does? In the Psalm it seems that in his life David had reached a point where there was no one there for him and he desperately craved God's presence but God appeared slow to respond. Of course we know that God did take care of David at the right time. But this cry from Psalm 22 is also a prophecy pointing to the anguish of the Messiah. Later in the same passage the focus changes to reflect the crucifixion as David talks about his hands and feet being pierced. There is no record of that happening to David so this part of the psalm is a direct prophecy about the suffering of the Lord. Sometimes in the Psalms and elsewhere in the scriptures what appears to be a statement concerning the writer and the circumstances of his times is also a revelation of things to come. Like mountain peaks, when you scale the first peak it reveals that here is a higher peak still to be scaled. Therefore the opening words of Psalm 22 might well apply to David but they also are an indication of the desolation that Jesus experienced on the cross. In order to become the perfect sacrifice and pay the full price for sin He had to suffer, without even having the comforting presence of His Father as he died in pain, for the sins of the world.

Perhaps I am speaking today to someone who feels deserted by friends or family or even by God himself. It can be quite devastating but keep the faith and remember Luke. 22 31. "Satan has received permission to test all of you"...We will be tested perhaps to show what we are made of and to display our trust, love, obedience, perseverance and also to stop us becoming puffed up with pride. Keep in mind the faith expressed in Psalm 27 14 "Trust in the Lord. Have faith, do not despair. Trust in the Lord"...and when we do, we come out of the trial with a stronger, firmer faith than before. The trial is our opportunity to grow.

Rest assured that the Lord will not abandon any of His people for ever. There was an old man who, every day, visited the care home where his wife, who suffered severe Alzheimer's, was a resident. One of the care workers said that it was remarkable that he came every day even though his wife did not know who he was any more. The old man replied "She doesn't know who I am but I know who she is". That's the faithful kind of love our Father in heaven has for us. He loves us even when we withhold our love from Him. If we listen to Him speak to us, we may hear Him say "You are my beloved child whom I will love forever."

Some people accuse Christians of using their faith as a crutch. If they mean it is something to help us on our walk through life, they are exactly correct. But everyone uses something to help them in their walk through life. Drugs, sex, alcohol, money, power etc. but we choose to rely on faith in the wisdom of the ages as proclaimed by the Almighty God in the Holy Bible. When faced with a choice why would anyone choose any other help? And if this is a crutch we can be confident in its use.

Yet there may come times when we experience dry spells in our Christian walk. When we do, let us not be discouraged but hold on, for our loving Father wants only what is best for us and in time and, with our co-operation and patience, that is what He will deliver.

ADAM AND EVE – FACT OR FABLE?

In describing the way in which God created the earth, the Bible tells a simple story which would be understandable to the people living at that time, people who had no more that a fundamental understanding of science and would certainly know little about quantum physics. It explains in uncomplicated language how earth, life, sin and the universe came to be.

One view of this scripture is that Adam and Eve are representations of the whole of humanity and that the first few chapters of Genesis are merely a figurative way of explaining how God created His universe. After all how could Adam who is described as the first man, live for 930 years and his children interbreed with no physical or mental defects?

Science has shown quite clearly that evolution has happened over millions of years culminating in the highest form of earthly life – mankind. Cro-Magnon man appears as the fully developed human that we could see on the streets today some 10,000 to 40,000 years ago while the Bible shows that the story of the first man, Adam, in the Bible goes back only 6,000 years. It would therefore seem clear that the Bible story of creation is just that – no more than a story. But there is another way of looking at this.

Firstly, if God created Adam, He would have created him genetically perfect which would explain why Adam was able to live so long and why his offspring could interbreed without any malformations.

Secondly, we see how the Old Testament writers were meticulous in recording ancestry and the Bible details the forebears of Abraham giving the age of each father at the birth of his first born son as follows:-

199

Abraham was born when his father, Terah was........ 70

Terah......................................Nahor...............29

Nahor ....Serug................30

Serug.....................................Reu 32

Reu..Peleg...............30

Peleg......................................Eber...............34

Eber.......................................Shelah.............30

Shelah................................. Arpachshad.......35

Arpachshad...........................Shem.............100

Shem......................................Noah.............500

Noah.....................................Lamech.........182

Lamech.................................Methuselah....187

Methuselah...........................Enoch.............65

Enoch....................................Jared.............162

Jared.....................................Mahalalel.........65

Mahalel.................................Kenan.............70

Kenan....................................Enosh. 90

Enosh.....................................Seth.. 105

Seth..Adam............130

Obviously Abraham must have had a real father whom the Bible tells us was Terah and in fact each of the men mentioned above must, of course, have had a real father. But if Adam is merely a myth , then which of these real fathers suddenly becomes mythical? Since this ancestral line is recorded so precisely it seems unlikely that the writer would change from fact to fiction with no indication or explanation, in which case the Bible is declaring that Adam is a real person and that Abraham is one of his descendants.

So if Adam is real does that mean we have to deny evolution? Of course not as the evidence for evolution having taken place is overwhelming but look at the possibilities. By the time that God created Adam the Cro-Magnons would certainly have spread to the area around the garden of Eden. Now we know that when Cain killed his brother he was banished from the land and he complained that the people who found him would kill him. What people? People who were living outside of the land from which he had been banished. Couldn't they have been the Cro-Magnons? And Cain married while he was banished so where did he find his wife? Most likely from those same people.

In Genesis chapter six we are told that the sons of God (or heavenly beings) saw that the daughters of mankind were beautiful and took them (as wives?). Now it is possible that the sons of God in this passage are the descendants of Adam (the first son of God) and the daughters of mankind are the descendants of the humanoid Cro-Magnons. The "heavenly beings" are more likely to be Adam's children than angels as we learn in the New Testament that angels do not marry and are, therefore, unlikely to reproduce. Therefore it is likely that the children of Adam could have interbred with the evolved race of humans.

This possibility brings science and the Bible together showing that they are not in conflict as is often claimed and indicates that God guided evolution to the stage where humans where formed and at that stage He created the ultimate human being in Adam who then was able to introduce into life on earth, the spiritual nature of Almighty God.

FATHER OR MOTHER GOD?

It is a curious fact that throughout the Old Testament no patriarch and no prophet ever called God, 'My Father'. The idea that God was our universal Father did not seem to be present in their minds. The only single human to be called His son in the O. T. was David when God said ' Today you have become my son and have I become your Father'. It was an isolated event. God may have wanted the Israelites to consider Him to be their Father but they were a stubborn and rebellious people who did not take that on board.

On occasions in the O.T. God is said to be like a mother in the way He cares but that does not make Him a mother any more than when He is said to want to take his people under the shelter of His wing, makes Him a hen.

The concept that God is our Father was emphasised by Jesus, a fact which is then is proclaimed throughout the New Testament. Did Jesus use the term Father rather than Mother to conform to the patriarchal society in which He lived? Unlikely on two fronts.

1. The Jews when they drifted away from God in the O.T. had no hesitation in worshipping false gods which included goddesses such as Asherah and Astartes in spite of being a heavily male dominated society. Their conventions or traditions did not prevent them honouring female deities..

2. When would Jesus ever allow convention or tradition to cause Him to disguise the truth? No when He called God His Father that was what He meant.

It is true that all the wonderful motherly (and fatherly) characteristics and qualities come from God but does that mean that God is both

Father and Mother? No, I believe that He has shown us the truth through human biology.

A baby's sex is determined by the chromosomes picked up from the parents. In creating a baby, one chromosome in each of the 23 pairs is picked up from each of the parents. The man has both the x and y chromosomes while the woman has two x chromosomes. If the x and y chromosomes are picked up then that baby is male. If there are two x chromosomes present then the baby is female. As the man has both x and y chromosomes, this means that the male parent has all the characteristics of both sexes residing in his body but that does not mean the he is both male and female and in the same way neither is God, who has all the male and female characteristics, both male and female.

When Jesus said 'Whoever has seen Me has seen the Father',who can say with certainty that He meant only in actions and character? He also said that when we pray we should say "My Father........"

Through the centuries God has been described as the Father. Nowadays we have introduced the idea of God being a Mother as well but this becomes a divisive issue within the churches. There are more than enough issues which divide the church already so let's eliminate this one and simply stop short of going beyond what Jesus instructs, and think of God as our Father.

THE HOMOSEXUAL QUESTION

The debate concerning the Christian attitude towards homosexuality is in danger of tearing the church apart. Arguments presented from both lobbies can sound equally convincing when the infallibility of the scriptures is called into question, or as it may be claimed presented in a way that is more in line with modern enlightenment.

Those who argue in favour of ordaining practising homosexual men and women to the ministry may claim that they are merely championing the human right to sexual fulfilment while those who object to it may state that their desire is to honour God's will as revealed in the Bible. It is a mistake however to brand all objectors as homophobes, for many do indeed have homosexual friends and family members who are loved for who they are whilst their sexual liaisons are not condoned.

The ministers of many denominations, when first ordained, make a confirmatory vow saying that they believe in the Westminster Confession of Faith which declares that the Holy Spirit speaks through the scriptures to be ' the supreme judge by which all controversies of religion are to be determined.' As that is the case let us try to understand what the guidance of the Holy Spirit is on this matter.

Firstly, it has been claimed that what the Bible has to say about homosexuality is vague, indecisive and inconsistent but the truth is that there are few things which are condemned as clearly and consistently as the homosexual act. This condemnation is in both the Old and New Testaments, the strongest point being in Leviticus 18 v. 22 where it says "God hates that". Of course the 'pro' lobby state that there are other practices prohibited in Leviticus which were forbidden at that time but which are not forbidden today, and in the light of that they ask: 'why then should we observe the restriction placed upon the homosexual practice and not the others?' Chapter 19 of Leviticus for example tells us that

1. We should not wear clothes of mixed materials (v. 19).

2. We should not cut the hair on the sides of our head (v. 27).

3. That fruit from the tree must not be eaten until the fifth year (v. 23-25).

Aren't these strange things to say? They seem to be curious instructions of no spiritual value whatsoever. So what is God telling us? In his great commentary, Matthew Henry explains point 1 above by saying that it was a heathen practice to wear clothes of mixed materials when they came to worship their God and that when we come to worship our Father in Heaven there is no need for us to adopt what the heathens do. Similarly, cutting the hair on the sides of the head was a heathen requirement and once again God is telling us that we should not do as the heathens do when we come to worship. Point 3 is answered by saying that in the first three years in the life of a tree, the fruit, if any, is of poor quality but in the fourth year when the tree has reached maturity, that fruit had to be dedicated to God. Thereafter the fruit was available to mankind. What this is telling us is that only the first and best is to be offered to God and that point, in conjunction with the explanation of the previous two points, is every bit as applicable today as it was when Leviticus was written.

Secondly, it is also pointed out that the New Testament does not condemn slavery and appears to uphold the subservient position of women and so as those attitudes no longer apply in today's world, doubt can be cast upon the validity of the condemnation of the homosexual act. But we must make the distinction between instructions issued to the people of that time for that time, and God's great moral law. Instructions to the people of that time may change. For example, because of the sacrifice of the Saviour we no longer need to sacrifice animals but....

God's great moral law does not change! It is eternal and mandatory for everyone.

It is also argued that in our more knowledgeable age we understand the true nature of human sexuality far better than the writers of the Bible. That is true but when we acknowledge that the Bible is God-breathed we cannot make a stand on that argument as God understands human nature better than the most erudite psychologist.

Many homosexuals claim that they were born that way but science has not detected any gene which can cause the condition and in any case even if people are born that way it is unlikely that they would be 'born again' into homosexuality. Being born again implies that we come to life in the Spirit and that things of a spiritual value are placed on a higher level than those of the physical.

The claim that God made homosexuals that way and therefore it is an acceptable practice is no more valid than saying that God made paedophiles and so that is an acceptable practice.

It is not the tendency towards homosexuality that is condemned any more than a tendency to lie or the propensity for pride. It is in the surrender to such temptations that sin is manifested. We must remember that we are living in a fallen world and that each one of us must take responsibility for our own inclinations and not blame God for the make-up of our character.

While it is said that Jesus Himself did not condemn the homosexual act, Paul did and he asserts that in speaking spiritual truths he was taught by the Spirit (see 1. Corinthians 2 :13 and Galatians 1 :11/12). However Jesus did say that the Creator made people male and female and for this reason a man would leave his father and mother and the two would become one. At no time did He commend homosexual union.

In fact Jesus does appear to condemn the homosexual act in Matthew 15: 19 where He declares that the things that make one unclean are "evil thoughts, murder, adultery, sexual immorality.........."(NIV) The Greek word translated as sexual immorality in this passage is "porneia" which Strong's dictionary defines as "fornication, homosexuality, lesbianism, sex with animals..." So the homosexual act does appear to be condemned even from the lips of Jesus Himself.

It has also been said that when two people love each other sincerely then it cannot be conceived that a loving God would withhold His blessing on them. God is a God of love and the love that people feel for each other is a gift from the Almighty but only when it can be measured against scripture. Two people in an adulterous relationship for example may claim that their feelings are sincere and wonderful but as it does not fit in with scripture they are mistaken if they think God will bless their adultery. The same can be said about homosexual love.

For centuries the Bible has been the building block of our faith so let us examine what it does actually say about the subject.

1. Levitcus 18. 22. No man is to have sexual relations with another man; God hates that.

2. Levitcus 20. 13. If a man has sexual relation with another man, they have done a disgusting thing.

3. Romans 1. 26-27... even the women pervert the natural use of their sex by unnatural acts. In the same way the men give up natural sexual relations with women and burn with passion for each other. Men do shameful things with each other.

4. 1. Cor. 6.9...people who are immoral or who worship idols or are adulterers or homosexual perverts...none of these will posses God's Kingdom.

That last quotation implies that practising homosexuals will not be part of the Kingdom unless they repent but if the church accepts homosexuality then it sends a message that there is no need to repent. In that case each vote in favour of condoning homosexual activity, must bear the responsibility of preventing practising homosexuals from the possibility of attaining the Kingdom of God.

Although we live in a so-called enlightened age can we be justified in disregarding the authority of the scriptures?

Perhaps the greatest need in today's society is for a heaven sent revival but won't God only send a revival when His church is willing to yield worldly wisdom and human attitudes to His Divine Will as revealed in His Holy Word?

We may have to live in a permissive society but God forbid that we have to worship in a permissive church.

JUDGE NOT?

One of the best known verses in the Bible comes in Jesus' sermon on the mount. It is often quoted to make a compassionate plea for tolerance. However there is more to this verse than there appears at first glance. The verse is *'Judge not that ye be not judged'.* Matthew 7 :1 *(*King James Bible*).* Now did Jesus really mean that we are not to judge whether or not a person's behaviour is good or bad? Are we not to judge if a Hitler or a Stalin is good or evil? Or if the actions of a paedophile are unacceptable?

What did Jesus teach the great evangelist, Paul? For it is clear that Paul got his instructions from Christ Himself. As it says in Galations 1 :11/12. *'Let me tell you, my brothers, that this gospel I preach is not of human origin. I did not receive it from any man, nor did anyone teach it to me. It was Jesus Christ himself who revealed it to me.'* There is evidence elsewhere in Paul's writing that his instructions came from our Lord. So did Paul make judgements? Of course he did. Almost all of his epistles to the early churches contain criticism of where Paul judged that they were going wrong and he instructed them on how they should correct the situation and sometimes he wrote with great power. For example in 1st Corinthians chapter 5 he highlights sexual immorality and says that the man who has done such a thing should be expelled from the fellowship. He declares in verse 11 that if a man calls himself a brother but is guilty of sin, the believers should not even sit down to eat with such a person. He then asks the question in verse 12/13 ' *Should we not judge the members of our own fellowship?'.* It is a rhetorical question meaning of course we should judge the members of our fellowship and why? In order to keep the fellowship pure, clean and to ensure that the standards that Christ demands are upheld.

Yet Jesus says 'Judge not'. Let's ask the question Did Jesus himself ever judge? Well He certainly did. Didn't He called the Pharisees a bunch of hypocrites and tell them that they were like whitewashed sepulchres, clean on the outside but full of corruption on the inside? Jesus was certainly no hypocrite and not the kind of man who would say 'do as I say not as I do'. So what did He mean when He said *'Judge not'?* The answer comes in the second part of the verse – *'that ye be not judged'* and the passage continues *'for the measure you use for others is the same measure God will use for you'*. It is an extension of the golden rule – do to others what you want them to do to you i.e. judge in the way you would want to be judged – not harshly but with compassion and love.

Martin Luther King once said that 'if we see evil and do nothing about it we become accomplices to that evil'. In the eyes of the law an accomplice shares the guilt with the perpetrator of the crime. Martin Luther King was a man steeped in the Bible and he probably had a passage from Ezekiel in mind when he made that statement. The Lord said to Ezekiel in chapter 3 that He was appointing Ezekiel to be a watchman for Israel and if he saw a man sinning and did not warn him to change his ways then God would hold Ezekiel responsible. So important was this instruction that God reminded Ezekiel years later as can be seen in Ezekiel chapter 33. In a sense we are all watchmen and therefore exercise judgement hence,if we do not warn and help those we recognise as having strayed from the path of salvation, then according to God's instruction to Ezekiel, their sin falls on our heads. Whenever a warning is thought to be necessary it is not to be given in a superior, holier than thou way, as if coming from an ivory tower but by drawing alongside the person with empathy for a fellow sinner. A wonderful example of this is seen in a man called C. Everett Koop who was a surgeon specialising in operating on children. He pioneered many surgical techniques and was so highly regarded that he was appointed Surgeon General to the United States at the time when Ronald Reagan was president. Dr. Koop was also a devout Christian and his appointment meant he had a political platform which threw him into the limelight. His stance on

211

being anti-abortion, anti-homosexuality and anti-smoking drew huge criticism from groups such as the Pro-choice, the Gay rights etc. But it was estimated that 20 million Americans stopped smoking because of the way he revealed the damaged that smoking did to the body and it was impossible to estimate how many lives of unborn babies were saved as a result of his stand against abortion. The American press slammed him asking 'who is he to tell us how to lead our lives' and called him 'Doctor unqualified'. Dr. Koop drew alongside the single mothers who were considering abortion and helped them in any way he could. His activities with the homosexuals were likewise filled with concern. When he eventually retired what a change had taken place. The newspapers issued an unprecedented apology for their early comments, the pro-choice group acknowledged him as a great man of the highest integrity and the gay rights movement also recognised that he loved the people while condemning what he perceived as their sin. He was awarded accolade after accolade and honoured with the Presidential Medal of Freedom which at that time was the highest civilian award that could be given by America. After he retired he remained friends with a man called Mel White who had AIDS as a result of homosexual activity. Once again he was criticised and was asked 'How can a Christian man like you be friends with a man like Mel White? Dr. Koop responded to the question by saying ' The real question is – How can a man like Mel White be friends with a sinner like me?' And there is the clue to guiding others. When we as Christians have to warm others of sin it must be done with compassion, love and kindness acknowledging that we too are sinners and that maybe we can help each other.

The statement of Jesus '*Judge not that ye be not judged*' was not intended to be used as an excuse for turning a blind eye to promiscuity but where judgement is necessary it should be carried out with compassion realising that as fellow sinners our goal should be to help each other stay on the path to salvation and to guide those who have lost their way, back onto the right road.

OUR AWESOME GOD

Bible Passages: Genesis ch25 v 21 - 34.

Ephesians ch2 v 1 – 9.

Our God is an awesome God! The God of all glory, might and majesty whose nature is far beyond the ability of human minds to fully comprehend. He is omnipresent. That is He is everywhere at one time not just on planet earth, but throughout the entire universe. As He tells us in Jeremiah 23 :23 'I am a God who is everywhere.' He is in the innermost workings of the atom and in the outermost reaches of space. He sees our every action. No darkness can hide us from God. There is no place we can go where God is not present. He walks with us through every storm that life throws up and tenderly cares for each one of us with love.

He is omniscient meaning that He knows all things. Every detail of our lives is known to Him, even our secret thoughts. The Bible tells us that even the very hairs on our heads have been counted. I remember some years ago talking about this very point with a friend who said that scripture didn't really mean that God actually does know how many hairs we have on our heads but it was simply a figurative way of illustrating God's extensive knowledge. I replied that if that was the case and if someone had sat down and counted the number of hairs on his head was it credible that that person would then have knowledge that God did not have? That is not possible. The Almighty already knows every thing there is to know. Everything is part of His creation and He knows everything intimately. When there are more than six billion people on the planet we are staggered to think that God can know all the details of all

213

those individual lives at every moment. The sheer magnitude of that knowledge may cause doubts to arise in our minds but that is because we are guilty of anthropomorphism, that is, attributing to God human characteristics and human limitations because with our limited understanding we simply cannot conceive just how amazingly infinite our God is.

Early in 2008 a super computer was installed in Edinburgh – I believe into the University there. The press reported that this machine could perform 63 thousand billion calculations in a single second. The radio report said that this was equivalent to every person on the planet simultaneously doing ten thousand calculations in one second. That achievement is way beyond our mental grasp but we accept it because we are talking about a computer. However our God is far, far superior to a man-made machine such as a computer, even a super computer, and is therefore capable of doing so much more. His capacity for holding knowledge is way beyond that of even the largest of computer hard drives. When the enormity of that fact is assimilated we can more readily accept that there is nothing in all of creation that God does not know, all the details of individual lives, all facts known to mankind and all those yet to be discovered. He is indeed omniscient.

He is also omnipotent. Yes, He is the God of absolute power, the God of creation who sustains the infinite expanse of space by His word. He is the God of mighty miracles which leave us spellbound. If you were to be asked 'What do you consider to be the greatest miracle that this almighty God ever did?' what would you say? If you were Jewish you might suggest that the parting of the Red Sea which enabled the children of Israel to escape from servitude imposed upon them by the Egyptians, was the greatest of the miracles. Here indeed is a mighty example of God's power as the Israelites passed through this sea on dry ground with walls of water on either side but when the chasing Egyptian army tried to capture them, in order to return them to bondage, the water engulfed the pursuers and they were destroyed.

Or perhaps you think that the miracles of Jesus were the greatest, maybe the healing of ten lepers at one time or giving sight to the man born blind, or the healing of the crippled man and then, of course there was the restoration to life of Lazarus. Yet again you could, no doubt, also suggest with some justification that the creation of the entire universe out of nothing was the greatest. There are many more we could consider, however there is one miracle that is greater than all of these and that is the miracle of providing the means of forgiveness for our sins! Why do I say that this is the greatest? It is because all the other miracles were brought about by the word of God. God simply said let it be and it was so. But forgiveness required the sacrifice of His only begotten son. Nothing was more demanding of God. Creating the universe, parting the Red Sea, healing all illnesses and even raising Lazarus from death, they were nothing in comparison to what it cost God to provide for the forgiveness of our sins. And you must realise what that means …..

the greatest miracle of all……… Was for you!!!

Whenever you ask for your sins to be forgiven you must be aware of what you are asking of God. It is something you must never do lightly and yet something you cannot afford to overlook. When you ask to be cleansed of your sins and do so sincerely you are asking for the sacrifice of Christ to be applied to you personally and you are accepting that you recognise Christ as not only your Saviour, but also your Lord.

The choice you have before you then, is either to carry on with normal self-absorbed living or to submit to the bidding of the Lord. If you choose the former you will enjoy earthly pleasures that have no eternal value but the latter choice allows you to become heirs to the riches of the Kingdom of Heaven. It is a decision which must be made

I am reminded of a program which aired on British TV entitled 'Deal or no Deal'. Towards the end of this program a contestant has chosen of one of two boxes. One of those boxes contains a prize that can be as much as £250,000 while the other has a much lesser value that may be as little as one penny. The contestant is not aware of the value in the box he has chosen and someone called the Banker offers to buy the box in the possession of the contestant for a price which is a lot less than the high value. The choice is; should they sell for what the Banker offers or hold on in the hope that the box they have contains the rich prize. When the right option is chosen there are celebrations and great joy but if the wrong choice is made there can be sadness and even, on occasions, tears.

Having to make the decision is certainly a cause of great tension but how much easier it would be if they knew which box contained the high value. Then they would be absolutely foolish if they chose the lesser value. The whole process is extremely nerve-wracking and full of nail-biting tension but do you realise that everyone throughout the entire world has to make a similar choice and with far greater consequences? Oh, we make choices all the time - what to eat, what to buy, which programs to listen to on the radio or watch on TV; the list is endless and these are relatively unimportant but there is one choice that is important above all the others. The joys of Heaven or the desire for passing pleasures is the choice that faces all of us; the things of eternal worth or those of no eternal value which will, in time, lead to 'wailing and gnashing of teeth'. But we have a great advantage over the contestants in 'Deal or No Deal' – we know which box contains the prize - it is the one marked 'Jesus' and it is available to all of us.

Yet there are many people outside the church and, no doubt, a few inside who reject this precious prize in favour of passing pleasure. Sometimes the shining bead seems better than the uncut diamond, the polished stone better than the pearl of great price. Indeed there are examples in scripture of such wrong choices being made. In our Old Testament Bible passage for example we see Esau selling his precious birthright as the first-born son in order to satisfy the pangs of hunger. This birthright carried with it great privileges and honour, but satisfying a physical appetite meant more to him than all that.

How he came to regret it later but by then it was too late. When a choice is made there is sometimes no going back.

At this moment you face a choice between two boxes. One has the shining bead of worldly pleasures the other has the inheritance of the riches of the Kingdom of Heaven. Your decision today may determine where are you going to spend eternity - either in the presence of the almighty God of love or in the torment of hell.

The salvation that is offered by Jesus cannot be bought nor can it be earned, it does not depend on how good you are, it is the gift of His Grace that can only be accepted through faith. As the New Testament reading says 'It is by grace you have been saved through faith. It is not the result of your own efforts but God's gift so that no one can boast about it.'

Can you afford to reject this free gift? To throw the saviour's sacrifice back in his face? Do worldly pleasures mean more to you than the joys of Heaven? I do not believe that there is anyone hearing the word of God who would reject the gift of Christ in favour of things that have no eternal value. Perhaps you have simply not got round to accepting the gift of salvation or maybe you think you should be more worthy and feel a little cleaner before coming to the Lord to accept His offer. I can tell you that you will never be worthy of this gift – no one ever is. It took the death of God's only begotten son to make it available to us. God wants you to come to him just as you are. He will do a better job of washing you clean than you could ever do yourself and when you submit to Him He will untangle every knot of sin from the tapestry of your life leaving you flawless and precious in His eyes. To delay is foolishness, procrastination is a tool of the devil and the choice is before you today. I strongly urge you to choose salvation.

CORRUPTION

Genesis 3:1 - 19, Matthew 23 :25-33

Today I want to look at the some of the wonderful privileges that God has given us but also at the way the power of evil that is Satan tries to corrupt them. Firstly let me ask a question – Do you believe in the devil? I do, but I have been surprised to learn that several men and women from various churches say they do not believe in the devil but that modern thinking says that he is merely a representation of a power of evil at work in the world.

We could spend hours arguing about our particular stand on matters such as this. So when such a question arises it is better not to rely on the wisdom of the age but to ask what Jesus believes and clearly the Bible tells us that Jesus without any doubt believed in the devil and the Saviour revealed that Satan was in complete opposition to the will of God the Father. Absolutely everything that comes from God is for our good and will be attacked by the devil in an attempt to ruin the harmony of righteousness.

Take television. TV is a wonderful invention bringing to us news instantly from all over the world and providing entertainment for all tastes. Programs explaining the mysteries of the universe, the stars and planets, unusual life on earth and the unfolding of the science of genetics etc. all bring great enjoyment, information and pleasure. But there is another side to television. Transmissions shown after the watershed of 9pm can be unsavoury in the extreme. It is so easy to find oneself tuned into a channel that contains material which should not be viewed by anyone with a basic sense of morality and especially not by Christians. You see Satan has a field day encouraging distasteful broadcasts to infiltrate our TV screens. That is one of the ways in which he works to corrupt something which is essentially good.

And consider the internet. In the past ten to fifteen years the internet has become a terrific and almost unlimited source of information where you can find details of just about anything. It has been calculated that if everything on the internet were to be printed in book form and the resulting books were piled one on top of another then there would be ten piles of books reaching from here to the sun. It is enormous.

Nowadays you can shop without leaving the house. You can email friends anywhere in the world at no cost and the mail arrives instantly. What an improvement over the post where it takes at least a day for a letter to be delivered and costs more and more.(in old money, at the time of writing, over twelve shillings to post a first class letter). I have one daughter who lives in Australia and I can talk to her and see her and my grandchildren on the computer screen live and free of charge for as long as we like by means of an internet application called Skype.

All wonderful but then we hear about cyber bullying and computer stalking and of course the readily available pornographic web sites. If you ever find yourself in such a site get out of it as quickly as possible for even people of the highest moral fibre can be caught in the grip of lewd thoughts and some have been found with hundreds or even thousands of photographs of child abuse and other pornography on their laptops. Every good gift that God gives to us will be subject to vilification from the adversary.

Just look at the wonder and beauty of creation as revealed in Genesis. God was pleased at each stage and said it was good. There in the garden of Eden, Adam and Eve were happy and content living in God's presence for they had only one restriction and that was that they were not eat the fruit of the tree of the knowledge of good and evil. And of course that was where the devil launched his attack and see how he did it.

He first of all cast doubt upon what God had said. 'Did he really say that?' One of the devil's ploys is to try to make us doubt the truth of God's word. When Jesus was tempted in the wilderness that ploy was the first line of attack that Satan tried when he said 'if your are really the son of God...' That word 'if" was designed to cause doubt about Christ's divinity but he could not introduce doubt into the mind of Christ and when confronted with each of the temptations that Satan employed Jesus replied with the words 'it is written' and he quoted the scriptures with full confidence that they were the true words of his father. The devil had no answer to that.

Even today after hundreds of years of being tried and tested the Bible still holds up against all the doubts and accusations thrown against it. One man has said that the Bible is the anvil which has worn out many a hammer of doubt. There is no other book that contains moral guidance in such abundance and for sheer sense and practicability it is unmatched anywhere in the annuls of literature. The reason for this is quite simply that it is the inspired word of God. Proved beyond any reasonable doubt by the number of Old Testament prophesies which were fulfilled in the New Testament and which continue to be effected today.

The second way that Satan tempted Eve was to imply that the Almighty had an ulterior motive and that the Lord did not want Adam and Eve to become equal to to himself. In this way the devil attempted to plant a seed of doubt about the goodness of the Creator.

In his temptations in the wilderness Jesus was shown all the kingdoms of the world in a moment and was told that if he would just bend down and worship the devil he would be given all of these. Now Satan knew that everything would eventually come to Jesus in any case but that, firstly, Jesus had to undergo the torture of crucifixion in order to pay the price for the sins of the world and he was suggesting that the Lord could be given the glory without the necessity of suffering that horrendous death. Perhaps he was trying to imply that God was cruel in allowing his son to take upon himself the sins of all mankind and that he, Satan, was a kinder option. But Jesus could see right through the lies and knew that the reason he came to earth was to redeem a people lost in their sins. The love that Jesus shared with the Father for his creation was shown in stark contrast to the self serving desires of malevolence.

But perhaps it was the final comment delivered to Eve in the garden of Eden which had the greatest influence. That was that in eating the forbidden fruit they would gain wisdom and knowledge. Now here was an appeal to something honourable. Wisdom and knowledge, surely traits that would be approved of by the creator, the very things that would protect mankind from error. But here is where we see the cunning craftiness of the devil. If he could make the pair on the ground value those qualities above their obedience to God's instructions, he would succeed in making them sin by disregarding the word of God.

He succeeded of course and Adam and Eve partook of the forbidden fruit and as a result Satan was able to open the door to introduce all sorts of evil into the world. According to the book of Genesis it was then that weeds and thorns started to grow. It was as a result of the fall from grace that women had to suffer great pain in childbirth and all through the centuries the whole planet has been buffeted by the whims of the evil one as it has experienced the consequences of original sin. It was that sin, of doubting God's word and His goodness and placing wisdom and knowledge on a higher plain than God's revealed will, which opened the Pandora's box of evil and corruption.

Satan's great triumph gave him the blueprint for his later plans in attacking all of humanity and it is something all of us must be aware of and guard against. If we are aware of it we can take steps to avoid being deceived by his three fold strategy.

1. He tries to cast doubt on God's word (did he really say that?).

2. He implies that God has an ulterior motive(he doesn't want you to become equal to him).

3. He appeals to higher qualities to encourage us to disregard God's word (wisdom and knowledge).

In order to neutralise these ploys we must

1. hold God's revealed will in the forefront of our minds and

2. understand that on the cross Christ showed how much God loves us and

3. realise that the father's purpose is always for our highest benefit and

4. even when we seek to exercise attributes of the highest nature we remain subject to His commands.

You may well ask 'is it possible that the devil can corrupt even our utilisation of God's gifts?' Can it be that we can even be encouraged to pervert the Godly gifts? Things like love, compassion, patience, humility and steadfastness are some of the fruits of the Holy Spirit but when these are exercised without regard to the will of God they can be misused.

As an example let's take one of the highest and most precious of God's gifts – that of love. If a married man or woman falls in love with someone other than their spouse and surrenders to that urge they may claim that they do so in the name of love but the scriptures say 'do not commit adultery' and therefore their action is sinful. Or look at a quality which is highly regarded and recommended for all Christians - compassion! Surely you may say it is not possible to overdo compassion. Shouldn't we always show compassion? Surely it is something we should display at all times. Even when confronted by sinners shouldn't we display loving compassion in the knowledge that Jesus died for their sins?

Jesus was without any doubt the epitome and the perfect example of compassion. But look at the way Jesus handled the situation with the Pharisees in our New Testament reading. Did He say ' Look men I know your are doing your best and that you have a message for the people and because of you and your ancestors the faith has been kept and handed down over the years. You have been introducing additional rules of your own making but I know your intentions are good so may God bless you in your ministry'.? No! He did not! In fact He told them that they were a brood of vipers!

Jesus, the most compassionate man who ever lived, realised that there is a time when compassion is overruled by correction and that time is when God's revealed will is being disregarded or abused. If our compassion causes us to excuse and even condone sinful behaviour then it could well be that such compassion is being subtly influenced by the evil one for as we have seen he likes to corrupt even the gifts of the Spirit.

Let no one think that he or she is immune to the subtleties of demonic influence for many a good person's reputation has been ruined by allowing a malevolent thought to disrupt an otherwise sound philosophy. Matt chapter 24 v 24 warns us that Satan will deceive even the very elect if that were possible. Maybe the elect come under stronger attack than those who already belong to the demonic kingdom.

In today's world we often see men and women behaving in ways that are diametrically opposed to the revealed will of God as recorded in scripture and we too must be on guard to ensure that our compassion is not being influenced to accept what God tells us is wrong.

The way to test it is to ask 'what does the scripture say?' and then to honour the most holy of all books instead of being deceived into thinking that our so called enlightened society knows better. If Jesus confronted the Pharisees in their error should we bend to embrace the violation of Divine revelation? I think not!

It's true that the devil is clever and cunning but if we place our trust in Jesus for our salvation and hold the word of God in our heart of hearts then with the power of the Holy Spirit we can overcome Satan's attacks and tell him to be gone.

SPIRITUAL REFRESHMENT THROUGH CANCER

I don't suppose anyone relishes the idea of being in hospital but in my case it brought about a time of spiritual refreshment. Being told I had a cancer and that an operation was necessary is not what I wanted to hear but the experience of that short stay in hospital left me feeling joy rather than despair.

Firstly the nurses really were angels. Nothing was too much trouble for them and one young girl in particular whose name was Sarah was amazing. She was so kind, thoughtful and friendly that I said to her on one occasion " Are you this pleasant at home?" to which she smiled and said "Well I try to be."

As the operation was being performed with a local anaesthetic I had hoped to be allowed home that day but perhaps because I was 80 year old and lived alone they decided to keep me in overnight and it was Sarah who was given the task of telling me. She said, almost apologetically, "I hope that isn't a problem for you." Jokingly I said "the only problem it gives me is that I didn't bring my toothbrush." She laughed and two minutes later she returned with a brand new toothbrush and a new tube of toothpaste telling me I could take them home with me.

Then after my operation she saw that my feet were bare and off she went to bring me a pair of slipper-socks saying "you can wear these to walk around the ward so you won't need to put your shoes on." On another occasion, as she passed my bed, she saw me texting on my mobile phone and she stopped and told me that if my phone needed to be charged she could get me a charger. It seems she was looking out for ways to be helpful not just doing what was needed. Sarah brought my meals to my bed on a tray and was always looking for ways to be of help. A little later I texted a friend to say "Hey, they are treating me like a Lord in here, do I have to go home tomorrow?"

Her attitude engendered a desire to respond in a similar way where I wanted to cause as little bother as possible and to help in any way I could and the thought came to me that if everyone could just behave in the same way as Sarah what a wonderful world this would be. We would all be looking out for each other and seeking each other's well being, being caring, friendly and compassionate. And then I thought isn't that the way it will be in Heaven? What a glorious thought! Perhaps we should spend more time contemplating the joys of the heavenly kingdom.

Secondly, thinking about pain; I was not in great pain as a result of the cancerous growth on my back, not unless I bumped it or leaned on it when asleep but when I was in the operating theatre the surgeon shook my hand. She looked like a young girl but appeared calm and confident and I felt assured that I was in good hands. However she told me that the injections would be very "sharp" and that I should not be afraid to shout out when the pain became too much. One of the nurses came over and held my hand and said "Squeeze my hand as hard you you can when it hurts." My immediate thought was that this was not going to be like getting a jab at the dentist. And it wasn't. The injections were more painful that I expected but I didn't shout out and when the nurse saw me grimacing she said "squeeze my hand." to which I replied "I don't want to hurt you" She smiled but the six injections were over in a fairly short time and after that I felt very little at all.

I was told that the surgeon had removed a cancerous tumour the size of a tennis ball from my back. It was wonderful being able to lie on my back again with no discomfort after the operation which had lasted an hour. Of course the anaesthetic wears of eventually and about ten o'clock that night the doctor came round and said he was going to give me two Paracetamol but I told him that I never take pain killers. He replied that he strongly recommended that I should take them but I told him that I could put up with a little pain. So he told me that they were there if I changed my mind. Well about midnight the anaesthetic had worn off completely and the pain from the wound was considerable. I put up with it for two hours trying to find a position to lie in where the pain would be eased but with no success. I realised that I was being stupid and buzzed for the nurse. She came right away and I said "those Paracetamol that I am not going to take? Can I take them now please?" She brought them quickly with a glass of water and I must say they did make a difference.

When I was being discharged the doctor told me that the pain from the wound would last for a week and gave me a week's supply of pain killers. Now although all that pain was far from pleasant I realised that it was necessary in order to remove the evil of cancer from my body and then I realised that there is a far greater pain – far greater than anything I suffered – a torturous pain that is unto death - and that is the pain necessary to remove the evil of sin from our bodies!!! But the glorious thought is this - that pain is not suffered by us because Jesus took that pain in His own body in our place. What a glorious Saviour!

I came out of hospital with a clearer awareness of the blessed Joys awaiting for us in Heaven where we will share Divine love with one another but also with a greater love and commitment towards the Saviour who suffered unbearable pain to pay the price for my sins, on a cross at Calvary.

And so I give thanks for my experience with cancer.

THE OLD TESTAMENT IN A NUTSHELL

Approx Time scale.

FROM 4000BC AND EARLIER.

BOOK – GENESIS.

In six days God created the earth and everything in it concluding with Adam and Eve and the garden of Eden. On the seventh day He rested. The fall from God's grace took place when Adam and Eve disobeyed God by eating the fruit of the one tree in the garden of Eden which was forbidden to them and as a result evil was allowed to afflict the earth.

Adam's first son, Cain, killed his younger brother, Abel, and was banished from the land. Generation after generation became more and more wicked and finally God decided to send a flood to destroy this wickedness. He told a righteous man named Noah to build a boat called an Ark which was large enough to hold a male and a female of every unclean animal and seven pairs of each bird and clean animals. When Noah and his family went into the Ark it rained for forty days and nights and all life outside the Ark was drowned. Noah and his family worshipped God, and when the flood subsided, his offspring quickly spread throughout the land.

However, many years later, a group of people decided to build a tower that would enable them to reach up to God and in a plain in Babylonia they built a city called Babel where the construction of the tower began. God was displeased with their arrogance and caused them all to speak in different languages so that they could not understand one another and in complete confusion the project was abandoned.

FROM 2100BC. After many years God made a covenant with a righteous man named Abram changing his name to Abraham and promising that his descendants would be given possession of the promised land. Abraham had a son called Ishmael by his wife's handmaiden who was named Hagar and 14 years later when he was 100 years old he had another son named Isaac this time to his wife, Sarah, who had believed she was beyond child bearing age. Although Isaac was the younger, he was chosen, by God, as the one to be given the inheritance. Because of a disagreement with Sarah, Ishmael and his mother were sent away feeling cheated. Ishmael became the father of the Arab race. This was the start of the conflict between the Arabs and the Jews. Isaac had twin sons called Esau(the first born) and Jacob who cheated Esau out of his birthright and blessing. Jacob had 12 sons who became the leaders of the twelve tribes of Israel.

FROM 1900BC. One of those sons, Joseph, was his father's favourite and had been given a coat of many colours which he treasured but his brothers were jealous and angry with him because of dreams he had which forecast that one day his whole family would bow down to him. When an opportunity arose they sold him into slavery in Egypt through a band of passing traders and told their father that Joseph had been killed by a wild animal. In Egypt, Joseph interpreted two of Pharaoh's dreams which told of seven years of plentiful harvests followed by seven years of famine and as a result he was assigned the task of storing the harvest during the good years and rationing it out during the famine. He became the second most powerful man in Egypt and he brought his family to live in choice land in Egypt.

FROM 1500BC.

BOOK - EXODUS

After about 400 years the Egyptian rulers had forgotten about Joseph and treated his descendants, the Hebrews, like slaves. A Hebrew named Moses had been adopted by the Pharaoh's daughter and when he grew up he saw an Egyptian mistreat a fellow Hebrew. He fought with him and killed him and fearing for his own safety he fled to Midian. Forty years later while still in Midian God spoke to him via a burning bush telling him to instruct the Pharaoh to release the Hebrew slaves. When Moses requested the release of the Hebrews, Pharaoh refused but God sent ten plagues over Egypt culminating in the death of the eldest son in each of the Egyptian families. The angel of death passed over the homes of the Hebrews. Distraught, Pharaoh let God's people go but soon had a change of heart. He sent his army to recapture the Hebrews.

However God parted the Red Sea and allowed His people to pass through the sea on dry land. When the Egyptian army followed them the sea came crashing down upon them causing them to be drowned. And so the Hebrew slaves were free.

BOOKS – EXODUS, LEVITICUS, NUMBERS, DEUTERONOMY.

The Lord led them into the wilderness promising that they would have a land of plenty but the Hebrews disobeyed God by not having the faith to enter the promised land at that time so they were made to wander through the wilderness for forty years during which time God supplied them with water to drink and manna to eat on a daily basis. Occasionally He also gave them quail for food. During this time God gave Moses the law and the ten commandments and instructed him on how to construct the Covenant box and the tabernacle which was a large tent where worship was to take place. Whenever God wanted them to move He went before them in a cloudy pillar by day and a column of fire by night.

FROM 1410BC.

BOOK – JOSHUA.

When Moses died aged 120, God appointed Joshua to lead His people into the promised land. Their first task was to cross the river Jordan. Although the river was in spate God halted the flow and enabled them to cross over on dry land. They captured their first city which was called Jericho. Gradually they took possession of the rest of the promised land and divided it amongst the twelve tribes.

BOOK JUDGES.

After the death of Joshua, there was a period of almost 350 years, when the people were ruled by judges such as Othniel, Deborah, Gideon, Jephthah and Samson.

BOOK – RUTH.

During this time a young Moabite girl named Ruth became a widow and lived with her mother-in-law, Naomi, in Moab. Naomi, who had lost her two sons and her husband was almost destitute. She decided to return to her home town of Bethlehem. Ruth showed great love and dedication to Naomi and insisted on going with her. While they were there Ruth met and married a wealthy man named Boaz. They were the great grandparents of king David.

FROM 1050BC.

BOOK – 1ST SAMUEL.

The Israelites became disillusioned with the judges and decided they wanted a king to rule over them like the countries around them. A prophet of God named Samuel who had been trained from an early age by the high priest Eli was told by God to anoint a man called Saul to be king. Saul ruled for forty years and had great success in battle but he did not always heed the Lord's instructions and so the Lord decided to make a young shepherd boy king in his place. The boy's name was David and he became one of the most successful kings being described as a man after God's own heart. While Saul was in power, David, still a young boy, fought and killed a giant of a man named Goliath and later became more acclaimed than Saul for his victories in battles against the Philistines. Saul in his jealousy became unbalanced and several times tried to kill David but David who had a special friendship with Saul's son Jonathan managed to escape each time. Saul was eventually killed in battle.

FROM 1010BC.

BOOKS - 2nd SAMUEL, 1st and 2nd KINGS, 1st and 2nd CHRONICLES.

It should be noted that the books of the Chronicles tell the same story as those in part of the books of Samuel and of Kings but from a different point of view.

David was devoted to God and wrote many of the psalms but while he was king, he had an adulterous affair with a woman called Bathsheba whose husband he then arranged to have killed in battle. When the prophet Nathan confronted him about this sin David immediately acknowledged it and said "I have sinned" but in spite of his repentance, the result of his sin was that his young son died. He married Bathsheba and they had another son called Solomon who became king after David, who by then had reigned for forty years.

FROM 970BC. Solomon was the king who built the temple in Jerusalem and was noted for his wisdom. Under his rule Israel became very rich and powerful. For most of his reign he was a Godly man but he married 700 wives and had 300 concubines who eventually influenced him to worship false gods which incurred God's displeasure.

FROM 930BC. On his death his son Rehoboam became king. He decided to impose heavy taxes on the people and there was a rebellion led by a man named Jeroboam. This was the start of the split in the Jewish kingdom with the northern kingdom, known as Israel, being composed of ten tribes and ruled by Jeroboam and the southern kingdom of Judah made up of the tribes of Judah and Benjamin under Rehoboam's rule.

Over the years there were 19 kings in Israel none of whom was pleasing to God while Judah had 21 kings several of whom were Godly men. Both kingdoms were guilty of introducing the worship of false gods and evil practices into their religious rites.

FROM 722BC. King Hoshea was the last of the kings of Israel as the Assyrian army under Shalmaneser invaded the northern kingdom taking all the Israelites back to Assyria as slaves. They became known as the ten lost tribes.

FROM 586BC. The kingdom of Judah lasted longer because of the righteous kings but their continual return to the worship of false gods led to the defeat of their final king, Zedekiah, at the hands of the

233

Babylonian ruler, Nebuchadnezzar. The temple was ruined, the walls of Jerusalem pulled down and the people taken captive back to Babylonia. So started the time of the exile.

BOOK – LAMENTATIONS.

This book is a collection of five poems lamenting the destruction of the beautiful city of Jerusalem and the glorious temple while recognising that the Babylonians were merely the human agents of divine justice. It points to the need to trust God and gives hope for the future.

FROM 1010BC.

BOOKS – 1st and 2nd KINGS , ISAIAH, JEREMIAH, EZEKIEL.

Throughout the time of the kings, there were prophets who proclaimed God's message warning them not to turn to foreign gods but to worship the Lord God Almighty alone. Great early prophets such as Elijah followed by Elisha performed amazing miracles; for example both raised children from the dead.

Elijah was was taken up to heaven in a whirlwind without tasting death and Elisha continued the work of encouraging the people to be faithful to the true God.

Isaiah's ministry took place over a very long period of time and he is especially known for his prophecy of the coming of the Messiah whom he predicted would be born to a virgin and would be called Immanuel – 'God with us'. Jeremiah was placed in a muddy pit for some days because his warnings of destruction were unpalatable to the king and Ezekiel was shown several visions including the valley where dry bones were brought to life.

FROM 720BC.

BOOKS – THE 12 MINOR PROPHETS.

The reason for calling these prophets 'minor' is simply because their books are shorter than the others.

These books come at the end of the Old Testament and include the well known book of Jonah. Jonah had been told by God to go to the wicked city of Nineveh in order to warn them to change their ways but he decided to get on a boat going in a different direction. A fierce storm arose and Jonah was thrown into the sea where he was swallowed by a large fish. After three days, in answer to prayer, the fish spewed Jonah up onto a beach where God repeated his command to go to Nineveh. This time Jonah obeyed and preached his message with such power that the people of Nineveh repented and were spared.

The prediction that the Saviour would be born in Bethlehem appears in the book of Micah.

FROM 539BC.

BOOKS – EZRA AND NEHEMIAH.

In the year 539BC king Cyrus of Persia captured Babylon and in his first year in that country gave permission for some Jews to return to Jerusalem with instructions to rebuild the temple. Some 50,000 Jews returned to their homeland and the work on the temple began. Opposition to this work caused the re-construction to be stopped but later under king Darius it was completed. Several years later, around 458BC., Ezra a priest and scholar returned to Jerusalem and re-established scriptural law and re-introduced sacred worship. In the year 444BC. Nehemiah, king Artaxerxes's wine steward was given permission to go to Jerusalem. In spite of great opposition he succeeded in having the walls of Jerusalem rebuilt.

FROM 550BC.

BOOK - DANIEL .

While the tribes were still in exile Daniel and three of his fellow Jews, Shadrach, Messach and Abednego were serving in the court of king Nebuchadnezzar. When Daniel's three friends refused to worship a gold statue they were thrown into a furnace but to the amazement of the king they were not burned up. Later under king Darius an order was given that for thirty days no one was allowed to ask anything of any God, only of the king. When Daniel continued to pray to the true God he was thrown into a pit of hungry lions as punishment but the following morning Daniel emerged unscathed. The book of Daniel also contains a prophecy of the fall and rise of succeeding kingdoms with amazing accuracy and pinpoints the time of the coming of the Messiah.

FROM 460BC.

BOOK – ESTHER.

Esther was a beautiful Jewish girl exiled in Babylon, at that time called Persia, in the days of king Xerxes. She was chosen to be queen in place of the dethroned queen Vashti. An evil man named Haman plotted to have all the Jews killed and deceived the king into signing a decree to that effect. The cousin (or in some translations, the uncle) of Esther, a man called Mordecai, discovered this plot and requested Esther to persuade the king to revoke the decree. Esther asked all her people to fast and pray for three days after which time she approached the king. This was a dangerous thing to do as the king could put to death anyone who came into his presence without being summoned. However the king asked Esther what she wanted. She suggested that she would like the king and Haman to come to a banquet that night. The king agreed and Esther said that she would like to do the same again on the following night. At the second banquet Esther revealed that Haman was planning to kill all of her people. The king in a fury left the room and Haman threw himself on Esther pleading for mercy. When the king returned he thought that Haman was trying to rape Esther and had him sentenced to death. The decree, to kill the Jews, could not be cancelled but the king allowed the Jews to defend themselves which they did successfully.

BOOK – JOB.

The exact time scale of this book is unknown but Job was a righteous man whom the devil used to tease God by saying that Job was faithful only because he was wealthy. God knew that Job would not waver and so He granted the devil his wish - to test Job. As a result Job lost all his family and all his riches and eventually his health but never his faith. He had three friends who tried to comfort him, in vain. A fourth younger friend joined them. All four tried to tell Job that his misfortunes were as a result of his sins and that he should repent. Job, however knew that he had always honoured God and that he had nothing of which to repent. Although he complained, he refused to deny his faith in God and in the end the devil was put in his place and God gave Job the same number of children as he had before and rewarded him with twice the abundance of riches that he had lost.

FROM 1000BC.

BOOKS – PSALMS, PROVERBS, ECCLESIASTES, AND SONG OF SONGS.

Many of the 150 psalms were written by king David and amongst the most well known is psalm 23 'The Lord is my shepherd'. It is a wonderful book containing worship, prayer, complaint, praise and a whole gamut of human emotions. The shortest chapter in the Bible is psalm 117 and the longest is psalm 119. Psalm 118 is the chapter at the centre of the Bible.

Proverbs was written by king Solomon and reveals the wisdom needed to live a successful and moral life.

For the most part Ecclesiastes is a depressing book as it tells of the futility of life but in the end it says 'after all this there is only one thing to say, - have reverence for God and obey His commands'.

Song of Songs is a series of love poems depicting the love that God has for His people and, as Christians claim, the love that Christ has for His church. It is attributed to king Solomon.

After the rebuilding of the temple and the restoration of Jerusalem there is a period of some 400 years during which there is no prophetic word from God. The scriptures called the Apocrypha which are not present in most Protestant Bibles record events between the time of the exile and the coming of Christ.

FALLACIES OF JEHOVAH'S WITNESSES

Their view:

1. *Jesus is not God..* Check John 1 : 1. and the footnote even in their own Bible declares He is 'divine'. In Isaiah 9 : 6 Jesus' name is Mighty God, Eternal Father....In John 20 : 28 Thomas confesses Him as God and Jesus does not contradict him. In Hebrews 1 : 8 the Father addresses Jesus as God. (The JW Bible changes this but all Christian Bibles concur). The Bible says God created all things and Jesus is described as the creator. In Revelation 1:8 God tells us that He is the Alpha and the Omega and in 22:13 Jesus continues His revelation to John by saying that He is the Alpha and the Omega. So there is little doubt that Jesus is in fact God.

2. *They insist on using the name Jehovah instead of LORD.* Most other Bibles use LORD rather than God's name from the belief that God's name is too sacred to be used commonly. In fact God says His name is Yahweh in Exodus 3 : 14/15. If someone says his name is Giovanni he would be insulted if you called him John. Since they are so pedantic, on this matter,they should use the name Yahweh and call themselves Yahweh's Witnesses.

3. *Jesus is the archangel Michael.* In Daniel 10 : 13 Michael is shown to be just 'one of the foremost princes.' Jesus is so much more than 'just one of many' he is unique.

4. *No blood transfusions are allowed* - based on the food instruction that we must not eat blood, but look at Matthew 12 : 1 – 4. This tells us that when the body's needs are great, the law regarding what must not be eaten may be relaxed.

Therefore when the body is in great need of a blood transfusion, such a procedure is not only acceptable but sensible.

5. *We must not celebrate Christmas*. This is based on the fact that the date was originally that of a pagan festival. When we consider how often pagans have tried to corrupt the great blessings from God, it is wonderfully refreshing to think that God has taken a pagan date, reclaimed it, and presented us with the opportunity to celebrate the most amazing event in human history – the coming to earth of God's only begotten son. It is incredibly insensitive to choose not to remember, rejoice and celebrate that most wonderful gift from our Father God.

6. *When we die we are completely unconscious until the resurrection*. Matthew 22 : 32 tells us that He is the God of the living which includes the spirits of the dead patriarchs. Also Jesus tells us the parable of the rich man and Lazarus in Luke 16 : 19/31 where the dead are able to talk and think. Check out 1 Peter 3 : 18/20 where He preached to spirits of the dead - not angels. In Luke23: 39/43 the thief would be with Jesus that very day in Paradise. Paul says that he would prefer to die in order to be with Jesus. He obviously knew that he would be aware of Christ after death as reported in Philippians 1 : 22/26.

7. *Christ's resurrected body was purely spiritual and had no flesh and bone*s. In John 20 : 27 Jesus showed that He had a body which still bore evidence of the wounds from which He died. In Luke 24 : 38/39, He clearly has a body of flesh and bones. The resurrection body is physical but with a new spiritual dimension.

8. *Daniel interpreted a dream which revealed that Christ would become king in the heavenly kingdom in 1914*. This dream is in Daniel chapter 4 and when the whole chapter is read the

meaning of the dream is explained clearly and in full and is fulfilled in king Nebuchadnezzar. It has nothing to do with Christ's reigning in Heaven. As they often do the JWs have put a spin on the scriptures which is simply not there. To claim that Christ came to rule in Heaven in 1914 cannot be correct as in Ephesians 1 :19/23 we are told that Christ reigned in Heaven at that time i.e. in the first century. Also see Mt. 28 18.

9. *Do not get involved in politics.* If righteous men are to avoid guiding the affairs of the world who will control the well-being of the people? The JW attitude is playing into the hands of Satan allowing him to have "carte blanche."

WHY WAS JESUS BAPTISED?

John the Baptist was calling people to be baptised for the repentance and forgiveness of sins and he attracted crowds of people of all categories. When some Pharisees and Sadducees came to him he told them that they were a bunch of snakes but it is surprising that the Pharisees came to be baptised in any case as they were the authorised interpreters of Moses' law. However, the word "baptise" does not appear in the Old Testament at all. Not even once. So there was no law concerning baptism

Perhaps they thought that this was a cheap way to have their sins remitted. Instead of having to sacrifice an animal from their herds, which the law demanded, they thought they could simply be immersed in water and be forgiven for any sin they had committed. But the Baptist saw through their deviousness and told them they were a bunch of snakes.

John had told the crowds that someone was coming after him who was far greater than he was and when Jesus came to be baptised, John recognised him as the Messiah and was reluctant to baptise Christ as he felt inferior and inadequate. However Jesus said "Let it be this way for now to fulfil all righteousness". That phrase can mean 'to fulfil the righteous demands of the law'. But as we have already seen there was no law regarding baptism and Jesus had no need to repent and have sins forgiven as he was without sin. So why did he feel he had to be baptised? Some scholars suggest it was to set the example for us but there is much more to it than that.

In the Old Testament the law required that for sins to be forgiven an animal had to be sacrificed. There were many such sacrifices but the most important was that of the atonement for the sins of the nation. In this case two goats were offered. The first (the innocent goat) was

242

put to death to pay the price of the nation's sins. The high priest then placed his hands on the head of the second goat and symbolically transferred the sins of the nation onto that goat which was then driven off into the dessert.

Before the high priest could officiate at this atonement the law demanded that must have a bath; see Leviticus 16 :4. Only then was he permitted to offer the atoning sacrifice.

In the book of Hebrews we are reminded that Jesus is our great high priest who offered the ultimate atonement of his own body. Just as the Old Testament high priest, in order to fulfil the righteous demands of the law, had to be immersed in water before offering the atoning sacrifice, so our great high priest fulfilled the righteous demands of the law by being symbolically immersed in water by John the Baptist to enable him to make the complete atonement at a later date.

Jesus was not baptised to have his sins remitted but to satisfy the requirements of the law pertaining to the high priest, prior to making the atonement for the sins of the world.

THE LUCKIEST PEOPLE ON EARTH

We, Christians, are the luckiest people on earth. What a wonderful, gloriously, enlightening Gospel message we have. It tells of a God who loves us so much that He gave His son to die in order to bring us into His presence. How unique is Christianity amongst the confusion of religious faiths that cover the globe. And yet there have been movements of religious thought which attempt to bring different faiths together as equals and sometimes that idea has been tolerated, accepted and even adopted by schools of thought within the Christian church itself.

In the latter part of the last century in a church called St Martins in the fields in London a service was held in which Hindus, Buddhists, Muslims and Christians came together in an act of worship, each group reading extracts of sacred scripture from their own faith. (Tripitaka, Bhagavad Gita, Qur'an and the Holy Bible). This united service was hailed as a milestone of co-operation and progress in the field of religious tolerance. Years later there was a movement which promoted the idea that all faiths are of equal value. While it is true that there is excellent guidance for good living in most faiths, it is a betrayal of Christ for us to place other faiths on the same level as Christianity.

Indeed, if we, as Christians, truly believe that God Almighty sent His Son to pay the price of sin by suffering a horrific death on the cross we must ask ourselves these questions. 1. If there was any other way to salvation would God have asked His only begotten Son to die in that agonising manner? 2. Can a person really call himself a Christian if he believes other faiths are just as good as Christianity? If other faiths are equally effective in providing salvation, Christ's death was unnecessary! We could have used the principles of those other faiths in its place. No there is no other way. Christ is God's only gate to heaven. Christianity is uniquely and wonderfully above all other faiths.

Mahatma Gandhi once said "You Christians don't know you are sitting on dynamite which could blow the world apart." and that he loved Christ but he did not see the evidence of Christian living in many people who profess to be Christians. He also said that he lived the message of Christ within his Hindu faith. Yes, people of any faith can attempt to engage with the moral codes of Christ no matter what faith they adopt. But Christianity is much, much more than simply living out moral codes. It also involves surrendering to Christ, it's about having Him live through us, accepting and trusting in His sacrifice for our salvation. Adherents to other faiths may have good moral codes but they do not have a God who died to cleanse them of their sins. In Romans 3 : 23 it says "All have sinned and come short of the glory of God." Those sins, leave a stain on the soul and Heaven will not permit sin-stained souls to enter in. Only by the blood of Christ are our souls washed clean of the stain of sin. We are truly the luckiest people on earth.

We are also lucky in the way we are blessed with the power of prayer. I have been reading a book about Demos Shakarian the man who founded a Christian organisation called The Full Gospel Businessman's Fellowship International. In this book he shows, time after time, the miraculous way in which God answers prayer. The book is full of miraculous happenings which came about in answer to heart felt prayer. On one occasion, for example, he was in Hamburg a few years after the second world war and he heard the story of a pastor who had been preaching in his church during the war. As he preached, the sirens sounded and the allied aircraft started to drop their bombs. The pastor immediately ushered everyone into their allocated bomb shelter where they heard the bombs exploding all around them. Eventually after what seemed like an eternity the 'all clear' sounded.

The pastor tried to prise open the metal doors by pushing against them but they were red hot as a result of the pounding they had taken. He found some wooden planks and levered them against the doors but the doors would not budge. The heat of the bomb blasts had fused the doors together. They were trapped and the oxygen level was falling fast. The pastor asked everyone to kneel down and join him in prayer. "Lord", he began "we know that you are stronger than the power of death. Father we ask you for a miracle. Open these doors and release us." After a short time they heard the dreaded sound of another aeroplane and once again they heard the scream of a bomb. The bomb landed close, very close. Not close enough to injured the trapped worshippers but close enough to blast open the fused doors. The pastor and his congregation filed out of the shelter and gave thanks to God for their rescue.

Almost every page of this book tells of amazing events which occur too often to be described as anything other than miraculous, as God answered their prayers. The power of prayer is not only for special people it is there for ordinary believers too.

Let me ask you a question. Do you feel that your prayers go unheeded? You pray for things and nothing happens? You don't really expect to receive what you pray for? Is your prayer merely a vain hope? Don't you trust that He will answer? Perhaps you think that God has more important things on His mind and is not willing to devote His time and energy to you. Well that's wrong! Jesus told us that God cares for every aspect of our lives the great things and the small. He even said that God thinks of us so intimately that even the very hairs of our heads have been counted. So when we pray do we really have the trust to expect to get the answer we want?

One farming community in America was worried because it hadn't rained for months and they were in danger of losing their crops. So they decided to set a time when they would go to the top of a local high hill and pray for rain. The day came and the whole community gathered together and climbed the hill where their minister prayed fervently for rain. As they were descending it did start to rain and it was noticed that only one little girl had brought an umbrella. She really expected the prayer to be answered. Maybe that's the answer - really trust and expect your prayers to be answered! As we are told in Mk 11: 24. " When you pray and ask for something, believe that you have received it, and you will be given whatever you ask for," Believe, trust and expect an answer to your prayer no matter how big or small, and you may be surprised.

Our God is a great big God so don't hesitate to pray great big prayers. Jesus showed the way. He prayed and did big things always in accordance with His Father's will. That is our guide too. Always accept and act on the Father's will.

What Jesus did is the blueprint for our lives. The Bible tells us that we should try to reach the fullness of Christ in our own lives. This means attempting to act and to think as He did. In every situation we find ourselves in we should think and act like Him. Now doing that perfectly is too much to expect of most of us but when we realise that we are learning, developing, and growing, we are permitted to fall short at times. A concert pianist, for example, did not just decide to sit down at a piano one day and play like a master. No, he had to spend hours, days, months and years practising , making mistakes but developing until he reached the required standard. The same can be said of authors. They may aspire to write like Shakespeare but they need to put their thoughts onto paper time and time again and critically review their work in order to make progress. Athletes also need to spend a large portion of their lives going through gruelling training sessions in order to reach a high standard. As Christians, we too need to keep making every effort to apply Christian standards in all areas of our lives, sometimes failing but nevertheless, growing, keeping in mind how lucky we are in that we have the power of the Holy Spirit to help us to be the best we can be. And with His influence we are urged to use the gifts He gives in the service of the Lord. That is the way to attain the fullness of Christ in our lives.

An evangelist called Ravi Zakarious tells a story of a boy who was asked to use his talents. What had happened was that a young homeless man had died and the minister who was to conduct the burial service realised that there would be very few people, if any, at the graveside. He asked a young member to his congregation whom he knew played the bagpipes if he would play at the burial service. The young man was happy to oblige. But on the day of the service the young man was delayed in traffic and turned up at the cemetery late, after everyone had gone except two men with shovels standing over the hole in the ground. The young man, however, felt he had agreed to play the bagpipes and decided he would honour the commitment and so he started to play Amazing Grace. He played as he had never played before, with such emotion that even the two men put their shovels down and stood reverently with their heads bowed. He felt it was the best he had ever played. When he had finished he packed up his bagpipes and left. The two men just stood there amazed. One said "That was amazing I have never heard anything like that before" and the other replied "Neither have I and I've been digging these cesspits for twenty years!" You see even when it seems that we are using our talents in vain, it does not go unnoticed. 1 Corinthians 15: 58 "Nothing you do in the Lord's service is ever in vain". No prayer you offer, no encouraging word you say , no act of kindness will ever go unnoticed by God. The Gospel tells us so.

Yes we are the luckiest people on earth when we make the the Gospel a major part of our lives. The Gospel is good news and it **is** good news for those who trust it's message but it is also bad news for those who reject it. We may not like to think about the wrath of God towards sin but the Bible does not disguise it. One Christian lady once told me she thought it was abhorrent to believe that God would cast anyone into hell. Yes, she's right and it was also so abhorrent to God that He took drastic action to enable people to avoid ending up in hell. He gave His son to die for us!

We like to think of God as being all compassionate and all loving but we must not forget that although God is always ready to forgive error he is not prepared to let the unrepentant get away with sin forever. The Bible warns of the wrath of God and there will be a time when His wrath, which is His antagonism against evil, will be displayed in all it's fullness e.g. Revelation 6:15 - 17. where those who come under God's judgement cry to the rocks and mountains to hide them. Hide them from what? Hide them from the wrath of the Lamb.

Nowadays the Christian message grinds against contemporary culture as the world has largely disregarded sin or even tried to make it sound appealing. A menu I saw in a restaurant for example described a dessert as "a sinful experience" and an advert for Bacardi Spice declared "who said the devil would come as a man?" A perfume was named "My Sin".Adultery is now called an extra marital affair. That doesn't sound too bad but it is still adultery and while the world may smile and accept sin as the norm, the church must make a stand against it. Modernity must not shape our understanding of sin. Scripture is to do that. I heard Rev Robert Morton preach one time and he said something similar which was very relevant to this message. He said "scripture must be determined by scripture." In other words do not let the trends in society shape our understanding of sin. Let scripture do that. The idea that men and women are sinners and need a Saviour may seem quaint to the people of the world but it must never be dismissed as quaint by those who belong to Christ's church. The words of another strong preacher Rev. R. Walker really hit the mark when he said "To tolerate that which scripture condemns is for the church to lose its moorings and to drift into a kind of moral relativism where **you** pick and choose what ethical standard you will follow." The folly of relying on human wisdom to determine what is right has been evident time and time again. Scripture on the other hand is God's infallible wisdom.

We are the luckiest people on earth in having the word of God to show us the acceptable ethical standards. In 2 Tim 3. 16 we are told..... "All scripture is inspired by God and is useful for teaching and correcting error".....

The word of God tells us what is right ....and you cannot go wrong by doing what is right.

WHO WROTE THE BOOK OF HEBREWS?

Traditionally, and for about 16 centuries, the book of Hebrews was attributed to Paul, indeed the King James version of the Bible entitles this book "The epistle of Paul the apostle to the Hebrews".

However several Bible scholars at various times have cast doubt upon the authorship of this book stating that Barnabas, Apollos, Priscilla , Clement of Rome or another follower of Christ could have been the author. In fact most modern Bible scholars today believe that the writer of this book is probably not Paul.

They quote :- a difference in style from Paul's other epistles and the fact that Paul always introduced himself as the author of his (13) epistles but the writer of Hebrews chose not to identify himself.

However,

> 1. If Paul is the author, then the difference in style can be explained by the fact that in his other epistles he is writing to people in churches who would have known him from personal experience as he had been instrumental in establishing and, or, building these churches which were composed of a large percentage of Gentiles. These Gentiles would have little knowledge of the great Jewish heroes who are extolled in the book of Hebrews. In this book he is writing to <u>Jewish</u> Christians who would know all about the mysterious man, Melchizedek, for example, a man of whom the Gentile Christians would have no knowledge. In the book of Hebrews Paul is free to write about things from a Jewish tradition and perspective and any change of style in his writing can be attributed to that fact.

2. Perhaps the reason Paul would not introduce himself as author in Hebrews is that he was writing to the Christian Jews, many of whom might not have met Paul personally. No doubt, however, that they would remember how Paul had persecuted the young church, which consisted at that time almost entirely of Jewish converts. The memory of the fear and dread experienced in those days, by his persecution, might cause them still to harbour negative feelings about him. He would not want the importance of his message to be diminished by doubt or grudge and, therefore, may have decided that it would be prudent to write anonymously.

Can a case be made that it was Paul who wrote the book of Hebrews? Yes it can. Consider the evidence,

1). Timothy was known to have a close, warm, almost familial relationship with Paul. It is significant that no other writer of an epistle mentions Timothy but in Hebrews he is described affectionately as "our brother." which is typical of Paul.

2). In every one of his epistles Paul always finishes somewhere in the last few verses by blessing the readers with 'Grace'. No other writer of an epistle does this. Not James nor the two epistles from Peter nor the three from John. Only Paul finishes in this way. How does Hebrews finish? "Grace be with you all." A strong indication that Paul may well be the author.

On the balance of probability, when everything is taken into consideration, there is a good case to be made that confirms, the statement in the King James Bible and the traditional view, that Paul is indeed the writer of the book of Hebrews.

MELCHIZEDEK– A MAN OF MYSTERY.

In biblical terms the time between Adam and Moses is about two and a half thousand years and what is strange, during that time, is that there is no mention of God's chosen people having a priest to conduct any kind of worship. There were priests in other parts of the country who worshipped false gods, in Egypt and Canaan for example, but not until the children of Israel were freed from slavery in Egypt did God establish the Aaronic also known as the Levitical priesthood among the descendants of Jacob. He did this through Moses and Aaron while the Israelites were in the wilderness, stipulating that priests should only be called from the tribe of Levi.

However long before Moses, the very first priest mentioned in the Bible is a mysterious man named Melchizedek to whom Abraham(called Abram at that time) offered tithes of the plunder he had won in defeating the four kings who had kidnapped Lot, his nephew and friend. Melchizedek showed he was greater than Abram by accepting his tithes and blessing him.

This Melchizedek is described as being the king of Salem which later became Jerusalem and he is called 'priest of the most high God'. It would seem then that there was a colony of unacknowledged people in Abram's time who worshipped the true God and who were situated in what is now known as the holy land. As this is so it is surprising that we don't read more of Melchizedek and this group of people in the Old Testament.

Amazingly God chose to make a covenant, not with Melchizedek nor with anyone from Salem but with Abram who lived in Haran in modern day Iraq and who came from a family of moon-god worshippers. God must have seen qualities in Abram which would make him the great patriarch of the Old Testament.

Melchizedek is mentioned only in Genesis chapter 14, Psalm 110 in the Old Testament and in Hebrews in the New Testament and it is in Hebrews that his mystery comes to the fore. In Chapter five of Hebrews, Jesus is confirmed as a priest for ever in the priestly order of Melchizedek. That would seem to indicate that this priesthood was of a higher status and more eternal than the Levitical priesthood. In chapter seven Melchizedek is described as the king of righteousness and the king of peace – titles we normally associate with Jesus. In the NIV it is also said that he was without father or mother, without genealogy, without beginning of days or end of life. This has led many to suspect that Melchizedek was in fact a pre-incarnation appearance of Jesus Christ.

We know that men have entertained angels without being aware and so it can be argued that the spirit of Jesus appeared in human form prior to His incarnation. However, there is another possibility and that is that Melchizedek could have been an angelic visitor to earth sent to influence Abram and to display the greater eternal priesthood long before Levi was born. That would explain his having no father or mother and no beginning or end.

A third possibility is that he was a normal, although specially blessed, human being and that the statement in Hebrews simply means that there was no *RECORD* of his birth, death or family but the reading of that passage makes that possibility sound unlikely.

We simply do not know for certain and may have to wait until we meet with Jesus in the heavenly world to discover the truth.

THREEFOLD DENIAL – THREEFOLD FORGIVENESS?

There appears to be a tendency in human nature to believe that we are better, stronger, more important and have greater integrity than is actually the case. Indeed Paul, in Romans 12: 3, warns us against this self- aggrandisement. "Do not think of yourself more highly than you should."

Even Peter, one of the greatest disciples fell prey to over estimating himself. During the last supper he told Jesus that he would never disown Him and that he was prepared to die for Him. Just a few hour later, however, he denied even knowing the Lord on three occasions. When he realised what he had done he went out and wept bitterly.

Later, after the resurrection, Jesus asked Peter three times if he loved Him and Peter responded by confessing his love, three times. Most Bible scholars consider this incident to be an indication that in confessing his love three times, Peter's threefold denial of Christ was negated and that could well be the case but there is a deeper meaning which is not often brought to light.

The first time Jesus asks "Do you love Me?" the word He uses for love is 'agape' which means unconditional, pure, selfless love. But Peter replies "You know I love you." However he does not use 'agape' but 'phileo' which is brotherly love. Perhaps he was being honest and realised that as he had denied Christ three times, his love was not up to the agape standard.

The second time Jesus asks "Do you love Me?" again He uses 'agape' and again Peter replies with 'phileo' - "Lord I love you like a brother."

Peter is upset when Jesus asks "Do you love Me?" on the third occasion. The reason might be that he is reminded of his threefold denial but perhaps there is another reason, because this time Jesus uses the word 'phileo' not 'agape' ie. - "Do you only love Me like a brother?" and Peter has to reply "Yes Lord I do love you like a brother." An acknowledgement that his love was less than Jesus deserved and a just reason to feel upset.

It seems that Peter was unable to declare agape love for Jesus at that time and he had the integrity to acknowledge that fact. Maybe agape love was a step too far at that time. However, years later when Peter is writing his epistles he instructs the believers to love God and, guess what - he uses the word 'agape'.(1 Peter 1:8 etc.). Peter has come to understand and share that agape love from and to God. What a wonderful and glorious experience it must have been when he finally had his eyes and heart opened to know what agape love really is.

LUKEWARM FAITH?

Isn't it wonderful to realise that God is a God of love? He cares for us in so many ways. He provides an hospitable planet to live upon; He gives us each day our daily bread; He rescued the Israelites from slavery in Egypt; parted the Red Sea; sent His son to pay the price for our sins and in so many other ways He shows that He cares and is interested in even the smallest events in our lives. "Even the hairs of your head have all been counted." Matt. 10: 30.

With a God like that we can be assured that He wants the best for everyone. We rest in the knowledge that our salvation is assured when we trust in His son for the forgiveness of our sins and so we are able to wear the righteousness of Christ as we stand in the presence of the Father. It is a joy to understand that this is what the Father wants us to do and so we are able to relax knowing that in Christ our sins are forgiven and are remembered no more.

However this joyful confidence ought not to be an excuse for resting on that assurance for we must guard against complacency and inactivity. God is a God of love but that is not His only characteristic. He is also a God of truth, beauty, righteousness and JUSTICE. He expects His followers to reveal His light to the world and is not pleased with lukewarm, inactive Christians. In Revelation chapter three the Laodicean church is told that because they were lukewarm they would be spewed out of His mouth. Harsh words such as these are often overlooked or even ignored in favour of the more comforting declarations from the Lord.

The tendency to focus on the things we find comforting and reassuring is part of human nature but if we go through the Bible with that attitude, building our understanding on the way we would like God to be and discount His more fearsome qualities, then we are building a faith, indeed a God, of our own making. The Bible has a word for that - idolatry!

How fierce and uncompromising is our God in dealing with sin. Here are three examples:

1. He sent a flood to destroy the whole of humanity, save eight persons, because of the evil in the world.

2. Because of the sins of the people of Amalek, King Saul was told to kill all their men, women, children , babies and animals.

3. He allowed His own people to be almost annihilated by the Assyrians and later by the Babylonians because they worshipped false Gods and were not true to Him.

It may be argued that as these events took place in Old Testament times they do not carry as much weight today but Jesus believed in those scriptures and often quoted from the book of Deuteronomy. The O.T. is God's dealings with His chosen people as revealed through His chosen prophets and its scriptures cannot simply be dismissed.

In the New Testament Ananias and Saphira were struck down dead when they sinned against the Holy Spirit. Jesus Himself did not compromise over sin; He told the Pharisees that they were hypocrites, clean on the outside but full of corruption on the inside, He formed a whip from some cords and chased the traders out of the forecourt of the temple and He was uncompromising with the Laodicean church in the passage from Revelation quoted above

Sin, in God's eyes, is a terrible thing but His love shows through in the way it is finally dealt with. As a God of justice, sin had a price that had to be paid and as humanity seemed unable to pay it, God made the heart breaking decision to pay the price Himself with the crucifixion of His only begotten son. It took nothing less than the death of His only begotten son to pay the price of our forgiveness.

When the degree of pain God experienced in order to give us the means of salvation is realised there should be no place for complacency. It becomes understandable that being lukewarm is not acceptable in His eyes. Every Christian man and woman ought to examine themselves in order to determine if the level of commitment to their faith goes beyond the tepid or if they really do love God with all their hearts and souls, with all their bodies and minds as Jesus instructs.

The question we must ask is this "Is the casual Christian really a Christian at all?"

Thanks be to God that He paid the price for our sins and that we can be forgiven for anything we have done or failed to do. The sacrificial gift of His Son is the most supreme gift we can receive and when we accept it we make a start on our walk of Christian faith which leads us, not to inactivity but to do the deeds He has prepared for us to do. See Ephesians 2: 10. "...good works which God prepared in advance for us to do." (NIV).

THE END

Printed in Great Britain
by Amazon